BREAKING UP WITH YOUR BREAKUP

A counterintuitive remedy
for heartbreak

Nicky Danks

First published in 2024
© 2024 by Nicky Danks, United Kingdom
Breaking Up with Your Breakup, Nicky Danks

ISBN print: 9798324559335

Created in conjunction with The Book Shelf Ltd:
Project editor: Ameesha Green
Editor: Shelby Jones
Proofreader: Gemma Rowlands
Cover designer: Niall Burgess and Rebecca Woods
Typesetter: Kyle Albuquerque

https://linktr.ee/TheLoveFix_With_Nick

DEDICATION

To everyone going through a romantic heartache.
A breakup is a terminal diagnosis that can
give you a new life. Don't waste it.

EPIGRAPH

Actions never lie, and words don't mean shit.

— Mark Manson

TABLE OF CONTENTS

INTRODUCTION

B reaking up with your breakup. What does this actually mean? I had no clue until I started writing this book—which didn't even begin life as a book but as a clever title for the YouTube content I was writing to appease our overlord, the YouTube algorithm. Then, the light bulb in my head flickered. I had half an idea. Now, it's rare that I even have half an idea, so hold on to your back teeth because I'm about to tell you that your heart will go on, only with a lot more swearing involved.

Tell me if the following sounds familiar:

All you think about from when you wake up to when you sleep is your ex. You dwell on how it ended; their facial expression when they said, "It's over", is burned into your memory, and you feel like no one else could know how you feel. You spend hours on YouTube watching videos on how to get your ex back, you talk to your friends and family about how you still have hope you'll get back together, and you literally put your life on hold.

Your family and friends, on the other hand, are praying for a quick death because you won't shut up about it.

By coaching hundreds of people through their breakups, I realised many become so focused on getting their exes back they form a toxic—and borderline narcissistic—relationship with the breakup itself. I think I can speak for you reading this. You don't much like that version of yourself. Your relationship with your breakup sucks, and it's very much one-sided and stopping you from finding relief from the breakup pain you never asked for.

Now, I say "you", but I have a confession: guilty as charged. Yes. Me! The holier-than-thou, up on my high-horse, dickhead writing a breakup recovery book about self-love, and personal responsibility, was once…

Just like *you*.

I spent the longest time in a relationship with my breakup. I spoke to anyone who would listen, and I practically completed YouTube. Every piece of content in the breakup space had the red viewed bar underneath it. I ran out of things to watch and was no closer to moving on. Watching this content didn't heal me. It kept me sick. And I felt even worse as time passed.

Time heals all wounds? No, mine was growing. I became angrier. I grew sadder. I blamed every man and his dog for how I felt.

This, my friends, is the issue almost every dumpee has. They do not take responsibility for their feelings or how they respond to their feelings, but I totally get why. You want your special person back, and your limbic brain demands you do something about it.

However, your logical brain is trying to reason and to get you to see the truth. Your special person left without consulting you, and you may never see them again. That type of pain is so savage that your limbic brain, or what we call the "feeling brain", doesn't want to hear the logic of your logical brain. That, my friends, is where things get messy. I hope this book can help you not miss the forest for the trees.

Trigger alert:

For this book to help you, I will say and examine things that will hit your pain points. If something here hits your pain point—I will be happy for you. I will consider it a job well done because you have taken the first step towards breaking up with your breakup and healing the wound which has festered for far too long.

I want you to consider that your ex dumping you isn't about you—it really isn't. Trying to understand their feelings, their approach to the breakup, and what led to it is a futile exercise without reward. Your ex binning you off is about their feelings and how they felt.

Your feelings are perfectly valid and justified. How you feel is *always* okay. However, the compassionate-but-hard-hitting truth of this book will give you the clarity you need to relieve that breakup pain.

Still with me? Kudos.

Most people do not wake up thinking leaving their partner is a good idea. Well, I suppose they must wake up one day thinking this is it, and that's why you're here with me. It's not a nefarious decision on their part but rather a choice whereby they knew it wasn't working for them, and they had to walk away.

Walking away. Left behind. Dumped.

Now, you must pick yourself up and take a new path.

Your biggest problem right now isn't that they broke your heart. They hurt your expectations. What you seek isn't meaning or understanding about your ex but clarity for your feelings and what to do now. Most of you will have tied so much of your identity to your ex that you have no idea who you are without them. You felt they understood you and thought you understood them, and "They would never leave me because they said they love me."

Yeah, well, you and me both, mate. We all got that part wrong and invested in what we thought was a sure thing.

When you invest too much of yourself in your partner, it becomes your entire identity. Breaking up is equivalent to losing a part of yourself and, subsequently, an emotional death. This leads to an identity crisis, which is why breakups can be so painful. So, you haven't just lost your relationship but also yourself!

Newsflash! You should not invest 100% into someone else—ever! You must only ever give 50% of yourself to any relationship. Keep 50% for yourself: career, hobbies, friends, family, and personal projects. So when a relationship does end, it still hurts, but you haven't lost who you are without them. You can function and put more effort into your career, hobbies, friends and family because you have already invested in those areas.

When our identity is threatened, it can feel like we'll die. Biologically, we've evolved to desire companionship because there is safety in numbers. Twelve thousand years ago, isolation meant death because natural predators would eat you. That's the same feeling we have with breakups, especially when we go all in. We don't have a natural predator anymore, but we still have that solid biological drive to be with someone, to be in a group where our identity is validated.

You must always maintain a sense of self to have a great relationship and preserve yourself should that relationship end.

I can only try to write a book that will lead you to heal, but your situation is unique, and so is mine. It would be ignorant as fuck to believe I could write a book which would get your ex back and magically solve your situation. But while I'm no wizard in this department, I am rather good at figuring out the patterns—the commonalities—occurring in most breakups.

Much of what you're about to read may be counter-intuitive. Actually, fuck that, this book will very much be counter-intuitive for most of you. If you're reading this, you likely know about my content through my YouTube channel, The Love Fix (a horrible name for a YouTube channel, I know, but when I first started my channel, I needed a name, and this is the best my unimaginative imagination could muster). My word smithery is about as artistic as a McDonald's Big Mac, but, like a Big Mac, you're getting what you asked for. Whether or not you enjoy it is also what makes me and that burger a bit too similar.

I started making content I needed to help deal with my breakup, and, I confess, I began focusing on trying to understand my ex and how to get my ex back. The more I read and learned, the more I realised I had no control over my ex.

What did I have control over? My thoughts and feelings. Once I understood this, I knew what I do now ensured what I would do tomorrow.

A different approach was needed, as Mark Manson says:

"Not giving a fuck does not mean being indifferent; it means being comfortable with being different... To not give a fuck about adversity, you must first give a fuck about something more important than adversity... Whether you realise it or not, you are always choosing what to give a fuck about."[1]

After one year of consuming breakup and ex-back content, I was still shackled to my ex. Then I read *The Subtle Art of Not Giving a Fuck* by Mark Manson, which changed my whole fucking outlook. The irony that a non-breakup book taught me more about breakups than an actual breakup book was not lost on me because it was the first time I was consuming content that made sense and made me feel better.

Let me break it down for you: The subtle art isn't about giving no fucks; it's about choosing when to give a fuck.

And, boy, was I placing my fucks in the wrong place. For me to not give a fuck about getting my ex back, I had to give a fuck about something else. So I started to give a fuck about getting *me* back. That is: levelling up, getting on my purpose, and breaking the fuck up with my toxic narcissistic relationship with my breakup.

Before we get into it. I'm an uneducated fuckhead from East London who swears too much. I am not an academic, doctor, or therapist. I hold no qualifications in this space except a master's in not bullshitting people. Therefore, there are no original ideas in this book and at the time of this edit, there are nearly four hundred swear words. I have taken what I consider to be the best advice from other books, applied it to getting over a breakup, and wrote the book I needed to read when I was going through a bad time. I am a big softy at heart, but I believe a true friend will always stab you in the front, not in the back. I will be your best friend throughout the journey of this book, and I will stab you in the front with my metaphorical knife into that metaphorical heartache of yours. It's not literal in a literary way.

I just read that last sentence and realised how fucked up it sounds. It's my book, I'm leaving it in. Go fuck yourself.

Just kidding.

I love you, really.

Under all my colourful language is a traumatised man who has undergone therapy and coaching to arrive at a point where I can say: "Fuck your ex and fuck trying to get them back." I'll be the first to admit I have been anxious and needy in my relationships because I did not know how to validate myself. And how would I know how to validate myself? That shit isn't taught in school, and it certainly isn't taught in the workplace. Yet, we have bullshit fairy tales telling us how relationships should work and that there is a happily ever after, but that's all they are—fairy tales! But more on these later.

As a child, I never felt right. I always felt… sick. My parents took me to the doctors but never found anything physically wrong with me (apart from a severe case of anaemia fixed with an iron supplement). But I ended up losing my appetite and throwing up. I didn't want to leave my room because I was terrified of the outside world. I didn't want to go to school. I didn't want to see my friends. And the more I hid, the more I tried to hide.

No one knew what was wrong with me, and it wasn't until I was in my 20s that I started to function a bit better, and it wasn't until my 30s that I realised what was wrong with me. I had chronic anxiety. As a kid, I never knew how to articulate anxiety. It came out like: "Mummy, my stomach hurts, and I don't want to eat anything."

I continue to battle anxiety now, but I know how to soothe my symptoms. Sometimes. When it does flare, I'm folded in two, paralysed. The only difference is I know what it is now, and I've learned the hard way to function with anxiety, which has led me to be quite dysfunctional.

Fucking ironic.

In the past, my biggest strength was also my biggest weakness. I was *functional*. At the height of my anxiety spirals, I could make it look like everything was okay. Of course, I was a tough man and didn't experience emotion. Right?

Wrong. It isn't easy to express your emotions when the social standard is to keep them to yourself. I didn't tell anyone how badly I was suffering until my mid-30s. I hid my anxiety in relationships for short periods before the mask became too heavy to hold on to my face. The emotional exhaustion would eventually overwhelm me, and I would become passive-aggressive, threatening silly things like: "If you don't tell me what is going on, I will leave." There wasn't anything going on; it was all in my head, and I was projecting my inner suffering outwards. These episodes were rare, but they did a lot of damage. My anxiety fed me false intelligence reports, making me insecure.

I am not excusing my behaviour. No, I am taking responsibility for it.

Learning to take responsibility for my life, no matter if someone fucked me over or if I fucked myself over, was the foundation of my breakup recovery. It is also in the foundations of this book. Anxiety no longer controls me. I no longer dwell on my ex. I do not attempt to control the uncontrollable.

Breakups are fucking amazing if you let them be. They can be the best opportunity of your life, and I do not want you to miss out. Your ex saying "No" means you can say "Yes" to everything you had to say "No" to when you were together.

Yes to no-contact. Yes, to holidays. Yes, to dating. Yes, to self-love. Yes, to self-care.

Before we go any further with the pep talk, I'll confess why I was dumped in the first place. Like most people in their mid-30s, I'd had enough relationships and breakups. I thought I knew what I was doing to feel settled and safe (remember: I have chronic anxiety, so this would've been one thing to worry about). So, determined and somewhat arrogant, I got with my ex, thinking I held the cheat codes to relationships and we'd never suffer a breakup again! Boy, was I wrong. Three years in (bear in mind I am in love and having fun), she turned and said: "I'm not feeling it anymore."

I want to say the breakup just happened, but that's bullshit. It had been building for a while, and the COVID-19 lockdown was the final nail in the coffin. And the simple answer was this: she no longer wanted a romantic relationship with me.

But why?

My anxiety spiralled. We were amazing. Our relationship was effortless. I felt like a great lover. I mean, I was nicknamed 'The Beast from the East'! Just kidding. Back to the book. I thought she was my forever relationship, my person. I loved her and her daughter with all my heart. I had been in love before, but not like this. We were compatible, and our chemistry was phenomenal. She was everything I looked for—so funny and feminine and… I still remember she'd say things so out of left field I would be on the floor laughing so hard I thought I was going to piss myself. I loved every moment. We had challenges like anyone else, but she was a very calm woman, so it didn't matter if I had a bad day or was pissed at something. One look from her and I was happy. Her beautiful brown eyes and radiant smile pierced me, and I was powerless. She had my number from the start, and I knew I was in trouble, but in a good way.

I took her to the New Forest on our first long weekend away together. We stayed in this beautiful, old rustic hotel with a secret garden like something from *The Lord of the Rings*. It was out-of-this-world breathtaking. We sat on a swinging chair in the heart of the heather and wildflowers, talking until the sun went down.

When you're in love with someone, everything is afire. Colours are vibrant, food tastes better—even toast tastes terrific—and you're high on feel-good neurotransmitters.

I knew then how deeply in love I was with her. I had never felt so safe. For the first time, I could be me. I was safe with her, and she was safe with me. So much so that she wanted me to be the father to her daughter—a true honour and privilege— but a significant issue later in our relationship. Most of our disagreements centred on this, alongside my battle with chronic anxiety and her avoidance.

Despite some challenges, she was the first woman to show me the difference between sex and intimacy. I was hooked and would've done anything for her and her daughter from then on. We got the little things right. We were more than okay with what we had, and if we didn't have money to go out, it didn't matter. We would sit indoors with homemade meals, listen to music, watch films, and talk. I wanted no other woman. I had my person. We were present with each other, which is the biggest thing I miss and what I find lacking in my dating experiences since.

Fast forward to late-2019 and early-2020. The COVID-19 pandemic exposed us. By Christmas, we had been living together for around 18 months and in a three-year relationship. For the most part, it was smooth sailing. I had moved into her place whilst my parents moved into my place after falling on hard times. My parents now live with me in my place because I am fortunate enough to be in a position where I can help support them. I appreciate this is a weird side tangent, but my parents have always been a source of strength for me; no matter how bad I've fucked up–they've been there. Giving back is a step on the road to breakup recovery. So, if you can help family or friends, I highly recommend it.

Returning to the pandemic lockdown, and I'll confess, my feelings for my ex were changing. By this point, her daughter was three years old, and I had become her father. Most of our conflicts were over raising her, my anxiety, and her avoidant attachment style. It didn't happen often, but over three years, it slowly chipped away at our relationship. I didn't realise how avoidant she could be until much later. When there was conflict, she would go quiet and shut down.

It's important to note there will be conflict in any relationship. I think it's a huge red flag when clients tell me: "We never fight." It is also a red flag when they say: "All we do is fight." All that means is there are no boundaries, poor communication, and conflict avoidance (this is unhealthy, I reiterate). Healthy relationships contain fights, but how you fight is important. Listening to understand, not to respond, whilst maintaining accountability and boundaries, is no small task. It takes time, patience and leaving your ego at the door. "I hear you" are the three most powerful words you can use in a relationship. Stop trying to 'win' arguments and find solutions.

Back then, I had enough knowledge to know that relationship issues must be discussed. Sadly, I often said, "Hey, we need to talk about this." And she'd say, "We don't need to talk about that." Sometimes, I'd talk for nearly an hour about the issue, and she would not respond. Everything was brushed under the carpet, and nothing was resolved. The issues with the baby got worse. I found myself in a world of: "It's my house; you just live here." And my opinions were not respected. She would frequently say: "Don't give the baby any snacks." The next thing I see is her and the baby on the sofa… eating snacks.

This was giving me the shits, and I was getting very annoyed. I felt like an outsider near the end. It was mother and daughter vs the stepdad. Don't get me wrong, I was no angel, and I got a lot of things wrong. My crippling anxiety had an impact on the relationship. I should have returned to therapy, but I thought I was on top of it. My ex should have also gone to therapy for her avoidant attachment style. We both had issues stemming from childhood, and we should have gone to couples therapy.

But we didn't.

By the end of 2019, I was so tired of feeling shut out that I wanted out. I felt like, at one point, I was paying bills and falling into a trap whereby I had to stick it out and continue to invest in my relationship emotionally and financially.

Enter March 2020: pandemic and lockdown. This is when things went to shit. Like most people, I was looking forward to not having to go into the office and getting paid for it. But, man, did that euphoria wear off quickly. Six weeks into the pandemic, the relationship was on the rocks. The pandemic wasn't the cause of the breakup, but it was the catalyst. I believe too much 'togetherness' is relationship rot, so ensuring you have a life away from the relationship is super important. Or else it becomes suffocating—poisonous and toxic to everyone involved.

Due to the pandemic, we didn't have a life outside of our relationship. This very soon exposed so many things I was not happy with. I stopped being such a nice guy and started to assert boundaries regarding certain things, but it was too late. I should have held these boundaries from the start, and maybe things would've been different, but we live and learn. When I started calling bullshit on many things in the house and the double standards with the baby, it caused colossal friction between my ex and me. It also highlighted incompatibilities that weren't comprisable. Due to my lack of boundaries, not handling my anxiety and not screening her correctly before starting a relationship, there was only one outcome—a breakup.

I was very quickly asked to leave and never returned.

That is the elementary version of events, and many more nuanced details could be a book on their own. But the gist is that the breakup led me to write this book, and breaking up with your breakup isn't an overnight deal but a process. I hope the following frameworks and examinations will give you the healing tools. How you feel is always okay, but how you respond is where the magic happens. You can still love your ex and desperately want them back. I don't care about that. I care about how you take responsibility for how you feel.

By improving your self-value and self-worth, you will see your breakup was the most significant opportunity of your life.

If I were to break down breaking up with your breakup into one sentence, I'd say:

A breakup is a terminal diagnosis that will give you a new life… if you allow it to.

This book will be compassionately brutal and sometimes trigger your pain points. I will be calling out your bullshit as well as my own. I will try to write this book a little differently, as in, I don't just want to give you a checklist of things to do to soothe your breakup. Whilst there are some unavoidable checklists in this book, I want you to see this book as a best friend with no filter who is telling you the truth. This kind of friend can be a dick, but they always have your best interests at heart. We will be breaking up with the breakup together. I say "we" because I will be with you every step of the way. But it is brutal… the act of questioning your identity so I will provide powerful tools to harness the power of the self.

I will give you a different attitude towards breakups. I will make you approach your breakup from a different angle. I will have you question why your relationships fail and why you must take responsibility for them and yourself—regardless of who caused the breakup. Responsibility will set you free and stand you on the path to growth and a better future where your relationships are stable and freeing, not debilitating.

This book is for you if you're tired of the 'get your ex back' bullshit because, let's face it, it hasn't worked, and you're done with the post-breakup mud you've been facing down in.

CHAPTER 1

Give Your Ex the Breakup

Your ex dumping you, no longer wanting romance, is their burden. Don't pick it up! Let them carry the weight of their decision. Give them what they want—the breakup—and let them have everything that comes with that. Give your ex the best gift of them all: your absence. Your burden is how you respond. Your burden is accepting the situation. Your burden is deciding what to do next.

It's the evening of December 10th, 1914, in downtown West Orange, New Jersey. A fire rages its way through the factory of Thomas Edison. The fire destroyed most of his inventions, prototypes, and designs, but Edison stood with his son while the firemen fought the flames and said: "Go get your mother and all her friends. They'll never see a fire like this again." When his son objected, Edison said, "It's okay, we've just got rid of a lot of rubbish".

What the fuck?

I can only imagine what the son was thinking, but what else could Edison do? Scream? Cry? Protest? Shit all over the floor like a baby? Or accept he has no control over the situation and plan his recovery. Consciously or otherwise, Edison was being stoic as fuck. Edison chose to see the burning down of his factory as a good thing. He was practicing *Amor Fati*, Which is Latin for "love your fate."

See everything in your life, good or bad, as an opportunity and a necessary evil to level up.

Edison, who was 67 in 1914, saw an opportunity to start fresh. Rather than licking his wounds, he got straight to work rebuilding his factory. Within six weeks, he was back up and running. That year, he made ten million in profit (about 200 million dollars today). The burden wasn't that his factory went up in flames. His burden was what happened next and how to only give a fuck about what he could control.

To quote Ryan Holiday from his book, *The Obstacle is the Way*:

"To do great things, we need to be able to endure tragedy and setbacks."

To be able to write this book and coach people through their breakups, I had to endure heartbreak, feelings of loneliness, anxiety, and worthlessness. But rather than shitting all over the floor and pleading with my ex, I eventually accepted the reality of my situation.

Amor Fati. Accept my fate, love the burden of recovery, and the opportunities it gives me.

Edison didn't get mad at the fire or cry, "Why me?" He accepted the fire for what it was—a force of nature he couldn't control. Like the fire, I had to accept my ex-girlfriend's decision for the force it was. She felt how she felt; she said what she said, and her fire was beyond my control.

What was the opportunity in my obstacle? In the context of the breakup, the opportunity was to give my ex precisely what she asked for: the breakup. This afforded me the wonderful opportunity to improve things I got wrong. The alternative was to shit all over the floor, beg and plead, further validating my ex's decision to break up with me.

My mindset from day one of my breakup was to give my ex as much space as possible. I didn't know what "no-contact" meant or how to handle a breakup. What I did know was that reaching out had never achieved anything in previous breakups, and I remembered how stifled I felt when a girl I'd dumped wouldn't leave me alone. I also like to think I was slightly more mature in my 30s than in my 20s, so it was time to put my big boy pants on.

With my big boy pants on came my big boy cry, and it was the ugliest cry of my life!

May 18th, 2020.

That was the official date of our breakup. After said breakup, I found myself to be technically homeless. Although I have owned my own house since 2014, I was living with my ex at the time. My parents and nephew had taken up residence in *my* house because they had fallen on hard times. It was a great arrangement because they were looking after the place for me. However, after I was unceremoniously dismissed from my ex-girlfriend's place, I had nowhere to go apart from the sofa in my house. I didn't want to throw my weight around and demand my place back. I had an agreement for them to be the stewards there. Just because my life was falling apart didn't mean I had the right to displace anyone.

I lived on my sofa for the next eight weeks with little to no privacy. I was surrounded by family, which was very much needed, but I felt like the loneliest person in the world. To quote Jean-Paul Sartre: "If you are lonely when you're alone, you are in bad company." I wasn't physically alone, but I was emotionally isolated because I had put everything into the relationship at the expense of myself. I was my own lousy company because I had outsourced everything in that context to my ex. I had no identity because the relationship was my identity. I quickly learned that putting 100% into a relationship meant I no longer had a relationship with myself.

It's a common mistake I see many make, but I understand why. When you don't love yourself and someone comes along who likes you, it's very easy to rely on them to give you meaning, purpose, love, and an identity. It feels great, and for a while, we feel whole. But it's literally the cost of ourselves we pay to avoid feeling alone.

July 18th, 2020—the day before the ugly cry. I had to return to my ex's place to collect my things. I decided to rent a place in London because I couldn't spend another fucking second on that sofa. I love my family but wanted to murder them because they were smiling too loudly. My friends Ryan and

Joe came with me to help get my stuff. It wasn't so much I needed help collecting things, it was more like a "we're not letting you go by yourself" kind of thing. I couldn't ask for two better pals. My ex decided she didn't want to be there, so she packed my things for me and left the key under the doormat. The surgical precision she had used to pack my things was savage. Everything from my underwear to the HDMI cables was packed. I think I knew then this was terminal, and she signed the death certificate on the relationship.

It hadn't quite hit me, but I was about to get skull-fucked by my emotions.

I took one last look around the place whilst fighting back a tear, reminiscing our great memories. I went upstairs to look at her daughter's bedroom one last time. I had spent so much time with her playing Barbie dolls, hide and seek, and silly made-up games I felt the need to have one last look. I'd helped raise her since she was three months old, and it hit me that I probably wouldn't ever see her again. I loved that little girl more than my own life. And this emotional knife was slicing me up on the inside. I said goodbye to her three cats, put the spare keys through the letterbox, and left.

As Ryan and I walked to the lift with the last of my things, I felt like I was watching myself from afar and thinking how sad it was that a genuine, loving, and healthy relationship had ended so easily. There wasn't enough room in my car, so we had to leave poor Joe in the nearby park, drive to my new place, drop off my things and come back to collect Joe. A nice bit of salt in the wound—having to return to where my ex lived just after I gathered my things. Ryan suggested that we grab some burgers and then go to the park. I didn't want to go, but it was a beautiful sunny day, and I thought I might as well start getting used to these things without my ex.

July 19th, 2020. Enter the ugly cry. I began to unpack my things and organise the bedroom in my new place. I remember

BREAKING UP WITH YOUR BREAKUP

unpacking with unparalleled efficiency and savagery. I was coming across many clothing items and trinkets my ex had given me over the years, and they were going straight into the bin. It was next-level scorched earth savagery. I finished unpacking and remembered the Formula 1 race was about to start. The race was at Silverstone in the UK (one of my favourites).

I looked forward to it all year, and there was no way I would miss one despite how bad I felt.

I planned to grab some food, enjoy the race, and kick back in my new place. My emotions had other plans, and, boy, did they fuck me up. Since the breakup, I hadn't processed what was happening. I still thought we might've worked things out, and I had unknowingly suppressed how I felt by keeping myself so busy. However, the second I sat down and realised the gravity of the situation, the floodgates opened, and the sheer violence of my emotions swept me away. I had the biggest ugly cry of my life—uncontrollable sobbing. I was rolling around, holding my stomach, punching my bed, cursing words that I'd never heard before, and, at one point, I screamed at the top of my lungs.

Fortunately, my new roommate was out. Otherwise, she may have feared for her life, which is a shame because I'm a fucking nice guy, albeit I swear a-fucking-lot. One hour later, I was still crying and missing Formula 1. Bastard! By this time, I had nothing left. I was all cried out. I recorded a voice journal and fell asleep. I had one of those dreams where everything was okay with the world, and my life hadn't been turned upside down. I started to get a glimpse of "real life" when my conscious brain started to awaken and remind me life is unfair at the best of times.

When I woke, it felt like someone had died. I had never felt so lonely in my life. My roommate was still out, and it was dark outside. All the lights were off, and I was in a foreign place with nothing familiar to comfort me. I would've given anything to hear my ex's voice or to feel her touch. I wanted to call and beg for her back, but just like Thomas Edison and the fire that wiped out his factory, I was determined to love my fate and get to work on rebuilding. Something stoic inside me told me not to invest my energy in someone who didn't want to invest in me.

The following day, my ex reached out, asking for help with the internet. I had a 1Gb full-fibre connection set-up there. It was fucking beautiful, and man, I was almost as upset to lose that as I was to lose my ex. I was back to the stone age, living like a troglodyte with a measly 100Mb. Fuming! I told her how to correct the internet issue and said the following:

"Thank you for helping with packing my things. I think I got everything and settled into my new place. I am sorry we couldn't work things out. I respect your decision to end our relationship, but I can't be your friend. Please only contact me if you want to reconcile."

She never replied.

At the time of revising this chapter, it is Monday 14th of November 2022, 10:33pm, and I should be getting my arse into bed. We've been in no-contact since my last text message to her. It has been a long time since I've considered this part of my life.

For researching this chapter, I reviewed my voice journals, and listening wasn't easy. It reminded me of a weaker version of myself and brought up some challenging memories. However, it also reminded me how far I'd come, and I think we can all agree that I fucking nailed it! I no longer think of myself as a victim of a breakup. I look back with curiosity and fondness. It set me on a path I never thought imaginable because I found myself writing this book.

I remember thinking how brutal it was. She never reached out or even asked how I was. Now I am like, duh! You told her not to reach out. I have also realised she was not required or obligated to reach out. She had her path, healing, and new journey to explore as much as I did. I have no doubt she views the breakup very differently to me, and that is okay. I have no idea if she monkey branched, rebounded or cheated, but at the end of the day, it doesn't matter.

All that matters is my acceptance of the situation and taking responsibility for how I feel and respond. Her dumping me wasn't an attack on me, nor did she hate me. It was a termination of our romantic relationship, which she felt was the best option for her. I took responsibility for my healing, growth, and the emergence of a new me. There was no screaming, shouting, drama, begging or pleading. I gave my ex what she asked for: the breakup.

My breakup gave me an excellent opportunity. I could say yes to other things because my ex said no. I could turn what I had to do into what I got to do. I got to fall in love with having the opportunity to be better. I could try to be like Edison and his factory burning down. He didn't see tragedy or heartbreak in his life going up in smoke. He saw an opportunity to go in a different direction and to improve.

We don't get to choose what happens to us, but we get to choose how we respond and feel about it.

Yes, breakups are savagely painful, but you can let that pain paralyse you or teach you: student or victim. Choose which one you want to be because one has a future for you, the other does not.

You can either lower yourself to a person you don't like who shat all over the floor. Or you can elevate yourself to someone who finds opportunity in heartbreak. Amor Fati. Love your fate, love where you are, and love your burdens. Take the opportunities they provide.

THE DEATH OF IDENTITY

Why are breakups so painful? Because they threaten your identity. When your identity is threatened, most people will project their feelings outward and avoid looking inward because it would mean questioning your identity.

> "The more something threatens your identity, the more you will avoid it."
>
> – Mark Manson, *The Subtle Art of Not Giving a Fuck*

Just like when we sustain a physical injury, the pain radiates away from the injury site. We do much the same with emotional pain because if we turn and face our inner pain, it's not the pain we fear but the version of ourselves we might meet when we look. Rather than asking questions like: "What did I get wrong?" and "How can I improve?" we exert emotional pain onto our exes.

Do the following questions sound familiar to you?

- Why did they do this to me?
- Why did they hurt me like this?
- Why did they leave when they said they would love me forever?
- Why do I feel I will die if I do not get them back?
- What did it mean when they said [insert generic bullshit line your ex gave you here]?

These questions merely redirect the pain away from you to project onto your ex. Rather than trying to understand yourself better, you're laser-focused on understanding your ex. Your identity is so tied into your relationship you'll create new and innovative mental gymnastics to hold onto what little connection is left.

Four words for you:

An exercise in futility.

The introduction mentions that most people invest their whole identity into a relationship. Fair and fucking obvious warning: the bigger the investment, the bigger the comedown! The comedown is so severe it can feel like you'll die if they leave.

Our whole lives, we're taught to do something to get something. Study hard to get good grades, tidy your room to get a new toy, work hard to get promoted, and so on. In the context of a breakup, this is terrible advice. If you were the dumper and wanted nothing more than to be away from the person you dumped, picture your ex showing up at your workplace with flowers, begging to get you back. Picture your ex waiting outside your front door for you to return home from work. Picture your ex calling your parents and asking them to convince you to stay. Would you find that sexy and romantic? Like fuck you would!

Don't be that person.

The dumpee is in full negotiation mode, trying desperately to prevent the event that will threaten their identity. This ties in with Manson's *Law of Avoidance*. You avoid the thing threatening your identity. You prevent the breakup by desperately trying to hold on to someone who has already slipped through your fingers.

What would happen if you agreed with your ex-partner's decision to dump you? What if you took responsibility for how you felt and responded differently? What if you did the most counterintuitive thing of all? Agree with them. Do nothing but vanish and heal yourself!

More on this later.

Let's try an alternative to Manson's Law of Avoidance. Let's create a law that can help you confront your breakup and see it as an opportunity to change your identity.

Let's call it *Nick's Law*.

How fucking original, right?

Nick's Law:

The breakup isn't about you, but it is your responsibility.

I said that to a client once, and they lost their shit, and I totally get why, but let me explain.

When your ex started dating you, they did what was best for them based on their feelings. Only you were okay with that because you wanted them as much as they wanted you. They validated you. When your ex decided to stop dating you, they did what was best for them based on their feelings. Only you were very much not okay with that because it wasn't something *you* wanted. This threatened your identity. On both occasions, they chose based on how *they* felt, not how *you* feel or what *you* think.

Therefore, breaking up with you concerns *their* feelings and what they think is best for *them*.

This leaves you heartbroken, but you have the job, duty, and responsibility to level up.

Having the ability, during phases of emotional turmoil, to view the breakup from your ex-partner's point of view is—for me—a great way to begin modifying your identity or, at the very least, to see things differently. Straight off the bat, you stop thinking about yourself and see how things might look from your ex-partner's version of reality. That's the beginning of a change in identity. I identify as someone who doesn't make my ex-partner's feelings for me *about* me, but I will take responsibility for how I respond to my feelings.

Exercise:

Put yourself in your ex-partner's shoes. Think about their life, world view, traumas, and past relationships. Do not project your thoughts, feelings, and how you think they should act. Focus on how they feel now, not what they felt when they first fell in love with you.

Would you have dumped you?

Trying to see things from your ex-partner's point of view can help you stop investing in someone who no longer invests in you. You can begin to accept your situation and identify as someone who practices self-love and self-validation and is not dependent on one person to be a village of people for you. You no longer identify as dependent on one person for their entire support system. You can build a new identity where you don't feel like you're suffering.

This isn't easy, and it takes time. Most people grossly underestimate how long it can take to feel normal again. The savage truth is that it took me 18 months to feel (somewhat) normal, two years to say, "I've got this", and three years to say, "I'm smashing it and loving my life."

Be kind to yourself and allow time to do its thing. Get over your ex correctly, not quickly.

I appreciate that you can only think about getting your ex back after a breakup. Trust me, I get it. For a whole year, YouTube would only recommend break up content to me.

#howtogetmyexback

The mental gymnastics you create for yourself are on another level, imagining every scenario to get your ex-partner back, to show them how much you've changed and how great you are. You're likely imagining where, when, and how this imaginary conversation will take place. Hell, I even imagined the exact clothes I would wear. Once again, you're desperately trying to return to where you felt safe. This is further perpetuated by an imagined future, which is not possible. This is terrifying but proof you must never fully invest yourself in one person.

To quote Gavin De Becker from his book *The Gift of Fear*:

"What you fear is rarely what you think you fear—it is what you link to fear. Take anything you have ever felt profound fear for and link it to each possible outcome. When it is real fear, it will either be in the presence of danger, or it will link to pain or death."

Or maybe it's the fear of the unknown. Of not finding another partner as good as your ex. Of them dating someone new and learning how to love and validate yourself. This is all linked to having your identity tied to your ex.

Identity is linked to emotional survival. Your emotional survival is linked to your ex, making them your safe place and primary survival tool. Your primary survival tool has left you. So, you have no identity, and you literally feel like you want to die.

#Idontknowhowicanlivewithoutthem

Exercise:

Think of ways you can create and diversify your new identity to help you break up with your breakup.

Example:

I, Nick, identify as someone who practices a healthy lifestyle by going to the gym and eating well. I, Nick, identify as a writer who creates YouTube content and (I guess now) and is writing this book. I, Nick, identify as someone who will love and accept his fate by accepting that events beyond my control are beyond my control. I can only control what I do, say, and feel. I, Nick, identify as someone who practises self-love and self-validation by not investing time in people who do not invest in me.

When you build your new identity, you'll quickly realise that you no longer identify as someone who clings to a breakup. You will start to identify as someone who appreciated the time spent with your ex, the memories, and the opportunity to say yes to new things and people because your ex gave you the gift of saying "No" to you.

Come Back With Your Shield, Or On It!

The typical breakup response is to feel shit, rejected, abandoned, degraded, shunned, and so on. Did you ever have that black hole of immense pain in the pit of your stomach that you hoped would swallow you whole so the pain would stop?

Yeah, me too!

Marcus Aurelius said,

"What stands in the way becomes the way."

NICK'S TRANSLATION:

Every obstacle presents us with a new opportunity we must embrace. This is excellently examined in Ryan Holiday's book, *The Obstacle is the Way*. The crazy thing is no one can make you feel a certain way. We can either respond in a way that helps us move forward or give in to it. How we respond ultimately determines how long we sit in our painful feelings. There is a time and a place to sit with our pain, as this can be a powerful lesson. For example, staying away from our ex after a breakup is painful, but it is a conscious choice and takes a lot of emotional strength to sit in the breakup mud.

Marcus Aurelius also said:

"You cannot be harmed if you choose not to be harmed."

My interpretation of this is that you can either choose to be a victim or you can choose to be a student. Realigning your mindset from, "How could they hurt me like this?" to "What lesson did this teach me?" is the difference between staying in the place that made you sick or finding the will to get better.

The Spartans spoke of a "beautiful death". A warrior either returned carrying their shield or laid upon it. Spartans would've rather died in battle, in a "beautiful death" than returned defeated or without their shield. If Spartans fled battle or lost their shield, they were shamed and demoted socially to the standing of a criminal. Cowardice was not tolerated.

Like shame is instilled upon a Spartan, most dumpees force it onto themselves. They take on the role assigned to them by their dumpers. They take on the role of the dumpee, which is the shitty part with shitty lines in a B-movie. You know that needy as fuck character who begs: "They were the one" and "All you need is love."

John Lennon can get fucked with *that* bullshit.

In a world of eight billion, we're compatible with many potential partners; the concept of "The One" is the biggest pile of Disney bullshit I will tear to shreds in the next chapter. Get that cancerous tumour out of your head right now.

Your ex was one of a million, not one in a million.

Either come back with your shield or on it. Have a beautiful breakup, just like the Spartans had a beautiful death. They had a straightforward choice to make: victory or death. Surrender or running away wasn't allowed. Your choice throughout your breakup is equally simple. Get yourself back or don't. A beautiful breakup is acceptance of the obstacle placed in front of you. It is rejecting the role of a dumpee. It is rejecting the victim mindset and embracing a student mindset. It is finding opportunity in the face of a life-altering event. Your ex dumping you is an opportunity. It is an opportunity to reflect, grow, explore, and pursue new projects. It is an opportunity to find allies amongst strange faces.

A breakup is a lesson that can only be taught through experience. What you do with that lesson is on you.

Student or victim?

Exercise:

Think of ways to avoid the role of the dumpee.

Example:

- I will not beg for them to come back
- I will not stalk their social media
- I will not make passive-aggressive posts on my social media
- I will allow myself to feel shit
- I will pursue new hobbies
- I will visit new places
- I will talk to that person I had a secret crush on

DUMPER VS DUMPEE: A TALE OF TWO MINDSETS

A breakup is a tale of two stories. It's a tale of opposites between the dumper story and the dumpee, which meet in the middle. In most cases, the dumper will experience the breakup pain at different stages to the dumpee. This normally occurs in the weeks and months leading up to the breakup because they no longer feel the relationship has a future, and their imagined future with the dumpee is slowly dissolving. The dumper will normally feel relief and freedom immediately post-breakup and, in many cases, start to miss the dumpee as the fading affect bias kicks in, typically within a few months.

In psychology, the Fading Affect Bias (FAB) is a phenomenon where we forget negative memories associated with a bad experience and only focus on our positive experiences. For example, falling off a bike and breaking your arm, but only remembering how much you love riding a bike. Or a family member steals from you, but you love them and forget how they fucked you over. Or your partner breaks up with you, but you remember all the fun memories.

After the dumper has ended the relationship, they are relieved. The weeks and months leading up to them having the courage to end the relationship are done. Ahh relief. They can relax. For the dumpee, it's just beginning. The feeling of your insides being hollowed out by a rusty ice cream scoop and the cold chill of your ex saying they no longer love you is just the beginning of a road less travelled. Depending on your personality type and attachment style, you may feel the pain instantly. Or… if you're like me, you feel a little shit, but then experience delayed shock that really hits you.

I'd much rather feel instant pain so I could respond appropriately.

Regardless of when the breakup hits you, the dumpee will go through the stages of grief, with the added pain of your ex still being alive. The mere possibility of them coming back is probably the most painful part for most dumpees. It would probably be less painful if your ex had passed away. When someone dies, there is a finality to it. It's a far worse event in your life, but I would argue the grief is a little easier to handle because you know they're not coming back.

My dog Kenzie was sadly put to sleep on the 31st of May 2022. Although I cried for four days straight, and I still very much think about him regularly, I was at peace with his passing far more easily than any breakup I've had. I'm not comparing my dog to a person, although he was way more fucking awesome than most people. But I knew I could never see him again.

With your ex, you're grieving someone who is still alive.

As long as you're both single and alive, that possibility will always exist in your mind, manufacturing false hope within you.

The dumpee's advantage over the dumper is that the dumpee is forced to adapt, improvise, and overcome almost immediately. The pain is so bad that it will motivate most people to put the steps in place to move towards relief. The dumpee adopts the no-contact rule (more on this later) and begins to construct a new identity. The dumper very seldom makes these types of changes. They feel they have the power and feel in control and that they did nothing wrong. Their relationship with you weighed them down, and now they are as light as a feather. At least until reality sets in and they start moving towards anxiety.

The dumper and dumpee are on a collision course. The dumper moves towards anxiety, and the dumpee moves towards relief.

After six months, the dumpee pictures a life without the dumper (albeit they still may be holding on to hope of a reconciliation). The dumpee has lost some weight, got fitter, started new hobbies, adopted a new look, etc. They are emerging and getting comfortable with being uncomfortable. The dumper may have eaten all their candy in one go, giving them short-term gain but long-term pain. Their single life isn't as good as they thought—their friends are suddenly unavailable, money is running out, and their rebound relationship isn't that great. This is where the fading affect bias might kick in, and their brain wants them to return to where they last felt safe, which was in a relationship with you.

The dumper and the dumpee are now at the breakup crossroads. The dumper is losing their power. And for the first time since the breakup, the dumpee has learnt to swim with the sharks and is doing okay. The irony is that the dumpee gave the dumper precisely what they wanted: the breakup! In most cases, the dumper will have second thoughts about the breakup and question their decision. Therefore, giving your ex the breakup will always work.

If your dumper comes back, it's because you gave them space; you worked on yourself and changed your identity, which massively improves your attraction. If they don't come back, then who gives a fuck? You levelled up anyway and got you back. Giving your ex the breakup is a win-win, so just fucking give them what they wished for and let them think happy thoughts forever.

With or without your ex, your train keeps moving. Of course, you want them on the train with you, but you will go along just fine without them, picking up new people along the way.

Take home points:

Amor Fati. Accept and love your fate. You can only control what you do, say, feel and think, so don't waste time figuring out your ex.

Breakups will always sting, but you can minimise the pain by diversifying your identity. Rather than giving 100% of yourself, give only 50%. Save pieces of yourself for yourself. Otherwise, the relationship will become your identity, shackling your emotional survival to it and your partner.

You'll have no identity if the relationship ends. This will feel like death.

Breakups can be fucking amazing if you let them be. Have a beautiful breakup. It will be the biggest and best opportunity of your life. Your ex saying no to you means you can say yes to other things.

The breakup isn't about you, but it is your responsibility. Your ex ended the romantic relationship with you based on their feelings, not how you felt. Nonetheless, you are responsible for using the breakup to your advantage and recovering: student or victim.

Choose wisely.

CHAPTER 2

How Disney Fucked Us All

Chapter conclusions normally go at the end of said chapter, but I will not even lube you up for this one.

Disney fucked us good!

Disney has us all believing we're entitled to a happily ever after without putting in any work. If you bought into this—like I did—like almost every other deluded dopamine junkie out there, it may be one of the key reasons your relationships keep ending. Disney removes all expectations of effort and replaces them with the narrative that love will magically find you, and the rest of your life will be a dopamine high. Due to how love influences our behaviour, it was considered an illness until the mid-seventeenth century.[2] As mammals, we possess something called the "neurobiology of behaviour" whereby our brains have an integrated reward circuit that transforms stimuli such as food, sex, and love into dopamine.[3] When neuroscientists scan our brains during these neurotransmissions of dopamine, I imagine love probably resembles a disease. We're as high as a kite on dopamine! Our hormones are all over the place, so we can't focus and lose our rationality and ability to sleep. We literally become delirious. It certainly checks a lot of boxes for a disease thus far.

I know that doesn't sound romantic, but knowing the facts may save your future relationships because you won't just expect them to work. I am not anti-love or anti-relationship, but I am anti-bullshit and anti-dogshit relationships. Believe it or not, long-term relationships can last if done right and if expectations are kept in check.

True love isn't what you experience in the first one to four years. True love is intentionally choosing your partner, even when the in-love feeling has worn off. True love means you're now in the service industry. Try not to ask what your partner can do for you, ask what you can do for your partner. If you service them without expecting anything in return, and they do the same for you, then everyone's needs will get met by default, and you will live happily ever after. I am not trying to get anyone to abandon love, but I am encouraging you to update your idea of love.

Therefore, if your ex left after the novelty wore off, then off they fucking fuck and let them have the Disney bullshit.

> "There is a difference between falling in love and being in love."
>
> — Logan Ury, *How to Not Die Alone*

Great book. Go check it out.

As much as I enjoyed Logan's book, I was horrified that chapter three is called: "Disney Lied To Us" and I had already submitted my first manuscript to my editor, thinking that at least this chapter of my book was a little bit original. I cried to myself that the same concept was in Logan's book. All jokes aside, I am amazed at how similar our thought processes are regarding this topic. Rather than crying about it and wishing the plague on someone I've never met, I think quoting her above rests my case.

Back to writing the book.

Your idea of love is underpinned by your biology. How you feel is led by your neurotransmitters making you feel a certain way, and your emotions, which essentially are a feedback mechanism, to interpret your external surroundings, and you call it love. Putting in the work to recognise the difference between falling in, and being in love is where the real magic can happen. After your Disney feelings for your partner inevitably normalise, you then must choose your partner. This shift in ideology regarding love is recommended because love doesn't *just* happen, the intensity of your love felt in year one, will likely be a shadow of what you feel in year ten and therefore love doesn't conquer all. We must be intentional with our efforts to adopt a growth mindset. Disney love is an ideology—a system that influences the economy and politics. All the films, books, and tv shows depicting Prince Charmings and princesses and love defeating evil are products to be sold. Stop buying!

Try to think of love as a paradigm shift, where societal beliefs and ideas change based on evidence and fact. There was a paradigm shift when we stopped believing love was an illness during the 17th century, transitioning into the 18th century belief the love was the by-product of a well-to-do courtship, shifting into the 19th century belief that love was sentimental displays of affection, and then the 20th century where love was tied to wealth and familial connections. Arrive in the 21st century, and love is a partnership between equals. However, how we approach love nowadays is twisted by a fucking myriad of ideas knotted by media corporations such as Disney.

It's not love at first sight. Lust, sometimes, but never love. We must grow to love someone. For example, take two single, average-looking people who start working together. There's no spark, and they act professionally with each other. Six months' worth of sitting next to each other, getting to know one another, sharing jokes, life stories, and so on, an affection grows. They find themselves texting often, hanging out on the weekend, and they start dating. It's less exciting and romantic than the Disney ideology of love. Still, it is far more sustainable and real, and they have a better chance of forming into intentional love after the dopamine levels out.

What a crazy concept—getting to know and screening someone before dating. Who would've thought?

Either by accident or design, Disney's romanticised ideologies give us a princess awoken by true love's kiss, falling in love at first sight with a half-woman, half-fish mutant, and an Arabian homeless boy who catfishes the princess of Agrabah. Aladdin was the original Tinder swindler!

Change my mind, I dare you.

The indoctrination of Disney ideology manifests in how we ultimately identify with love. It's hard to change because it has been shoved down our throats since childhood. Your identity is linked to your survival, which is evidence enough to tell you that love alone isn't enough and doesn't help you overcome challenges or obstacles.

A key tool in your breakup recovery will be to question your idea of love and your identity. Did you think you would fall in love with the one, and your feelings for them would never change? Did you think you would find your prince or princess, rescue them from their wicked stepmother, fall in love, and you would love them more and more every day? Apply that logic to anything else in your life. You might have the best job in the world, but do you love what you do every second of every day? Did you imagine yourself being in that job until the end of time? Did the possibility ever exist that you could lose that job? Did the possibility of you wanting to change jobs ever provoke an emotional reaction in you to change? Love very quickly stops being a feeling and becomes a choice. This is where the mind shift, or a change in your identity must take place. You can start by choosing your breakup, regardless of how much it hurts.

The changes you want lie in the discomfort you avoid.

Now, when fuckheads like me call into question your identity, which subsequently threatens your emotional survival, you may feel like going down swinging. I mean, really, a breakup is a pin in the bubble of this ideology because relationships aren't an eternal dopamine high. Limerence and love don't conquer all. While love is important to a relationship, it's not achieved at first sight or with minimum effort. Relationships

47

require numerous elements to succeed: trust, communication, compatibility, and shared values.

If you, who are reading this, still believe love does conquer all, please know you're fucking wrong. You may want to stop reading now because what is coming up will be brutal. But if you're willing to strap on a pair and walk with me, you may find a better way of dealing with a breakup and finding worthwhile relationships where expectations are kept in check.

Here's the thing. After one to four years, you will feel differently about your partner. After ten years, you will feel vastly different to how you feel now—assuming you can get that far. It's okay if you think I'm a fuckhead. I won't lose any sleep over it. But if you're sick and tired of your relationships ending because your idea of love is fucked, this version of you needs to die so the new version of you can have healthier relationships. The new version of you will see that your ex was one of a million, not in a million. You take them down from the pedestal and break up with your breakup.

THE ONE! WHATEVER THE FUCK THAT MEANS!

The concept of the one is based on mythology. It has no real-world application, and it is fucking stupid.

"According to Greek mythology, humans were originally created with four arms, four legs and a head with two faces. Fearing their power, Zeus split them into two separate parts, condemning them to spend their lives in search of their other halves."

— Plato, *The Symposium*

But I get how seductive it sounds. The one is mysterious. The one has the cheat codes to your heart. The one already knows and understands you. Therefore, you don't have to put the work in. The one is cut from the same cloth as you, and when you find them, you will be complete. That all sounds magical and alive with the glow of a million fairies, but the one is a lazy concept, and it is entitled.

Suppose you find yourself only feeling happy with a partner... If you can't be happy being single for long enough to work on yourself, your Disney script will always torpedo your relationships because you need attention. If you can be okay with being single for a whole year and doing the boring well, you may lower expectations of a new partner just enough to know that romance is not always lollipops and rainbows but quite mundane. Consider this. You want a super exciting romantic love story because your life is boring. You're seeking what is missing from your life and expecting it to solve all your problems. When the Disney excitement wears off, the real work will begin, and love must be a conscious choice to do the boring well. It's not something that just happens.

Time for another one of Nick's laws.

Nick's Law of Entitlement

You're entitled to love yourself unconditionally but not to unconditional love from a romantic partner.

Romantic love is *highly* conditional. It depends on your looks, personality, values, morals, and goals. For me, the concept of the one implies that romantic love is unconditional. Unconditional love, for me, implies you don't have to work on yourself. You're not special. I am not special. Your ex or future partner is not unique.

In a world of eight billion people, it is statistically improbable that you will only be aligned with one person, and what a

BREAKING UP WITH YOUR BREAKUP

fucking needle in a haystack job that would be. Assuming that most people are only compatible with 10% of all other human beings, you would have 800 million potential people compatible with you. Let's get even more extreme and say you're only compatible with 1% of all other human beings. That's still a whopping 80 million candidates.

To quote Joey from *Friends*, it's like saying: "There is only one flavor of ice cream." So, grab a spoon and try the world's different flavours. Pick the best balance for you and stick with it. Should that not work out, grab another spoon, and keep tasting until you get it right.

Thought experiment

If you believe in the one, then maybe you're entitled and a full-on narcissist. Or maybe you do not love yourself as much as you think because you want to outsource all love and validation from another.

What does the one actually look like?

- The one understands me.
- The one loves me for who I am.
- The one completes me.
- The one wants to do everything I want to do.
- The one is my destiny.

And what do you sound like?

- "When I meet the one, I'll just know it. I will feel that magical spark."
- "The one will fit my exact physical requirements; if they deviate from my requirements, they are not the one."

Me, me, fucking me. It's all about me and what the one can do for me. I dare you to tell me that isn't entitled narcissistic

CHAPTER 2: HOW DISNEY FUCKED US ALL

thinking. Change my mind. And don't worry, we'll get onto the idea of a spark and the rest of the bullshit in a bit.

Allow me to translate what the one, soulmates, lobsters, penguins, or whatever fucking term you have for it means.

NicksDictionary.com

soul mate

noun

1. I'm too fucking lazy and entitled to do the work on myself to get the relationship I want. I do not want to change anything about myself, and if my soul mate does not like that, then they are not the one:

   My soulmate will accept everything because everyone always tells me how great I am. I deserve love. I deserve the one. And the one will find me.

I refer you back to Nick's Law of Entitlement. You're entitled to love yourself unconditionally but not to jackshit from anyone else. Real, sustainable, tangible love takes constant work and a growth mindset. The concept of the one is an entitled victim mindset, and people with victim mindsets will attract victims.

People with a growth and student mindset will look inward and ask:

- "What am I doing that is causing my relationships to break down?"
- "What am I doing to prevent me from finding great romantic partners?"

If your ex had 'the one' mindset, fuck 'em off. Let them burn and let them think happy happy thoughts forever. They did you a favour because you will never be able to keep up with their unrealistic expectations, and they'll probably die alone. If you who are reading this has this mindset, cut the shit right now, otherwise, start buying cats because you will die alone.

If you don't want to die alone, then keep reading and hopefully, you'll swap this mindset for a growth mindset.

Think realistically:

> "My partner is a great balance for me. We perform relationship maintenance regularly and serve each other's needs by listening to understand, not responding, and evolving together."

REAL LIFE IS BORING AND THAT'S OKAY

Let's tear up the Disney script and examine what successful couples do right.

Outside of great communication and mutual respect, the most successful relationships do the boring and mundane well. It's an awareness that modern life is quite dull. Realistically, how exciting is your life? There is what we think it is, and there is reality.

> "Mastery requires practice, but the more you practice something, the more boring and routine it becomes. Once the beginner gains are made, and we learn what to expect, our interest begins to fade."
>
> James Clear, *Atomic Habits*

Tell me if the following sounds familiar:

You wake up at 6am, hit the gym, shower, get dressed, and jump on a train for an hour-long commute to work. You don't hate your job but don't love it either. Like most, you're working hard to pay for the shit you don't need, tolerating bullshit office politics and banter. You clock out at 5pm and power walk to the train station, later enduring a sweaty commute home. You cook dinner, catch up with your partner, spend two hours watching Netflix and seek validation on social media from people who wouldn't notice if you died. You go to bed and are too tired to have sex, so you sleep.

You wake up and do it all again.

This is real life, my broken-hearted friends. It's not some magical land where you have an abundance of joy. You will not wake up in love with your partner every day. After the honeymoon period, you won't want to fuck each other seven times a day. In fact, there will be days where you wake up and hate their stupid fucking face, their stupid fucking voice, their stupid fucking smile, how they brush their stupid fucking teeth because the stupid fucking toothpaste runs down their stupid fucking chin like a stupid fucking baby, trying to feed its stupid fucking face for the first fucking time. You're going to hate how fucking long they spend in the fucking stupid bathroom, doing stupid fucking shit, and taking way too fucking long to have a stupid fucking shower.

How many times did I say fucking there?

Answers on a postcard.

Disney + social media = manufactured happiness

Media curated by a user can make their perfectly imperfect, dull and normal life look anything but. When you're lying there at 11pm at night mindlessly scrolling Instagram, stressing because you must wake up at 6am for a job you're probably not crazy about, and asking yourself, "Why doesn't my life look like that?" know that your admiration for these people is misguided because their life doesn't look like that either. You're comparing your behind-the-scenes real-life mundanity to their manufactured bullshit highlight reel, disguising their real-life mundanity. When you can be okay doing nothing with your partner and not expecting them to fulfil your needs and soothe your insecurities, you will function how you need to.

You must also be okay with the honeymoon excitement going away and never coming back with your partner. That type of novelty only comes with someone new. Like buying a new phone or pair of shoes, the new shiny toy feeling will vanish because people are insidiously good at normalising everything. How quickly does the excitement for your new iPhone or pair of shoes wear off? By the time you've gotten used to your new gadgets or the feel of your trainers, a new version has been released anyway.

The spokes on the wheel of life are repetitive. They simply are. Still, that doesn't mean it's a bad thing. After the excitement wears away, you must *choose* to love your partner and put the fucking work in.

At the start of a relationship, it very seldom feels like work because you've got the Disney feels. When that is normalised, you must be intentional because that is where the real work will begin. What felt like an act of love is now a chore: buying flowers, visiting the in-laws, celebrating their successes, respecting their boundaries, and just showing up is no longer as fun as it used to be. The novelty is long gone. Doing the work means actively doing the things you no longer find novelty in. It's just like brushing your teeth. It's a chore, not a pleasure, nonetheless it's essential maintenance that must be done to ensure a healthy set of teeth. Relationships are no different.

> "You need just enough winning to experience satisfaction and just enough wanting to experience desire."
>
> James Clear, *Atomic Habits*

Can you imagine Disney animating a real relationship? Happily ever after would look something like this:

Everything is perfect for a while, but then the excitement wears off. Our characters start annoying each other. They have crisis talks and realise life is boring most of the time. Follow an ugly and undignified breakup. Our main character searches YouTube: How do I get my ex back? They click the channel—oh, that's me!

If you found my channel during your search, you're a fucking legend! Sadly, most people also pay for a love spell or program to get their ex back they're so desperate. Later on, they'll realise it's a load of bullshit and repeat this cycle another three times until they realise they can't live like this forever.

This truth is a hard sell, and I fully understand if you put the book down at this point. But I already have your money, so the joke is on you. In all seriousness, try and stick with me. I doubt this Disney dramatisation will do well in the Box Office because the truth is like poetry, and everyone fucking hates poetry.

If you and your ex conditioned each other to soothe one another's pain through distraction, then you may not love yourself as much as you think you do. Did you honestly screen each other long enough to ensure you were compatible, or were you still hurt from a previous relationship and or just lonely, and you hired them to distract you? Loving yourself often means abstaining a little longer than you are comfortable with, but that extra time is often the key to finding relationships that are sustainable, not just ones that are distracting you from the underlying pain.

To quote Logan Ury, "Great relationships are not discovered—they are built."

If you haven't tossed the book away, I will tell you that you're at a very important stage now. You've got a lot of work to do on yourself. And you're the common denominator in everything you do. You finally understand you need to change your definition of love. I know I am being about as subtle as a grenade, but I believe we all need a cold splash of water sometimes.

Relationships can be the best and worst feeling in the world. I genuinely want everyone to find happy and healthy relationships. Still, sadly, most people do not know what that looks like because we have romanticised romance, and it's killing our relationships.

Remember, we never see what happens *after* the happily ever after. That's because real life is fucking boring and mundane, and shit happens. It's okay for us but not for Disney and social media because it doesn't sell.

Just before my ex ended our romantic affiliation, we were six weeks into the COVID lockdown and were both ready to jump out the window because we were both blinking too loudly. Her daughter was doing what three-year-olds do and you could cut the tension in the house with a knife. At the end of a very long, irritating and stressful day, my ex asked me to take a selfie with her and her daughter. It was the most perfect picture you'll ever see. Of course, she uploaded it to social media, to get validation from people who wouldn't care if we died of COVID the following day. The amount of comments and likes we received were on another level. We received comments like "You're the perfect couple" to "What a beautiful happy family". I fucking hated that picture! All I kept thinking to myself was, if only you fucking knew the shit that happened before that picture was taken!

I so badly wanted to respond to those comments with the following. My stepdaughter had been a dick from the moment she woke up. That's okay because she was three and she couldn't go to nursery or to the park. Nonetheless, her screaming all day had been like someone taking a cheese grater to my brain. My partner wouldn't talk to me unless she needed something.

We hadn't been intimate for six weeks; she wouldn't hug me, we were arguing over silly things and I just wanted to cry.

How many likes would that have got on Facebook?

My point is people only post on social media to sell false versions of themselves. The same way the film industry sells us false versions of love and romance. Don't compare your real-life behind-the-scenes pain to someone else's fake highlight reel on social media.

Like Disney, it's nothing more than a fairy-tale.

LUST, ATTRACTION, AND ATTACHMENT. OH MY.

Dopamine is fucking awesome when it's in balance, but we unfortunately live in unbalanced times. We get a hit of dopamine when we're expecting a reward such as hyper-palatable foods, sex, alcohol, and so on. These feel-good activities are in immense abundance in the modern world. This abundance is causing a huge problem, especially in romantic relationships. It is the demise of many relationships because we do not have biology that is meant to have such frequent dopamine hits. Great-tasting fast-food can be delivered to your door, an array of alcohol can be bought at the bar, your television has every channel pre-downloaded, and there is certainly more than one way to get sex should you choose to.

It's a cycle of motivation, reward, and reinforcement. This ties in well with the Disney fantasy because everyone is super motivated when they fall in love. No task is too small, and no distance too far to be with "the one". Add to that amazing dates, with amazing food and amazing sex; you will be swimming in dopamine, feeling loved up to your eyeballs and having to buy a bigger waist size because, let's face it, we will put on a little happy weight when we're in the Disney fantasy. Enjoy this phase of a relationship. It is fucking amazing, and I will certainly make the most of it in my next relationship. However, the bigger the high, the bigger the crash, also known as "we've lost the spark" or "I love you, but I'm not in love with you". Translation: I want my dopamine high, and it's not as good with you anymore, so I will find a new source.

If we do not stay aware of the double-edged sword of dopamine, then we're not arming ourselves with the correct tools to maintain a relationship after the honeymoon phase.

When dopamine is in balance, it's a potent tool. It is essential for productivity and hardship. Think of something you've been working towards for a long time. Saving for a mortgage on a house, training for a marathon, or a yearlong project at work. You will get a surge of dopamine when that task has been completed. You will also get a dopamine hit when that activity makes you want to quit. Back in the day, out on the savagely cold plains, our ancestors would have to hunt their dinner, knowing they could get injured or die. It was a perilous activity, but the release of dopamine tuned us in to anticipating the feast to come. Therefore, it's not so much the thing we want; it is the anticipation of how it will make us feel.

> "It is the anticipation of a reward—not the fulfilment of it—that gets us to take action. Interestingly, the reward system that is activated in the brain when you receive a reward is the same system that is activated when you anticipate a reward."
>
> James Clear, *Atomic Habits*

This is why the Disney fantasy can be so powerful and short-circuit our long-term thinking. The anticipation of getting that falling-in-love feeling is a powerful voice, forever whispering,

"Remember how we used to feel? That shit was amazing. Sure, we have stability, security, and someone invested in us, but there's no spark, excitement, or fantasy. Our lives aren't as great as those we follow on social media. We want that. Let's go get that."

The anticipation of falling in love is what most really want. The anticipation of how you think you will feel keeps you searching for the mythical spark. Newsflash. Falling in love can only happen for the first time—one time only—with the person you're with. Your love can grow into a more realistic, long-term love, and that is when oxytocin will do its job (more on this coming up). But you will never get that intoxicating, high-on-dopamine Disney first love feeling again with the same person. You can either get comfortable with the fact that your idea of love and your ex-partner's idea of love is totally fucked and update your expectations accordingly; or you can repeat the same Disney love and breakup cycle, and I'll book you in for a breakup coaching session.

We have too many external stimuli, giving us constant hits of dopamine. Every time you get a notification on your phone, whenever someone likes something you posted on social media, and every time you get a match on Tinder, it will give you a hit of dopamine. We were only meant to get hits of dopamine sparingly, like when we would set out with our tribe to hunt dinner. The dopamine hits are so frequent and intense these days; not only do we need more and more to keep us at baseline, but we're essentially becoming resistant to it. It's called: 'Nothing Makes Me Happy Syndrome', but it short-circuits oxytocin, the long-term thinking neurotransmitter.

According to a team of scientists led by Dr. Helen Fisher, romantic love can be broken down into three categories: lust, attraction, and attachment.[4]

Each category is characterised by its hormones stemming from the brain:

Lust = Testosterone and Estrogen

Attraction = Dopamine, Norepinephrine, and Serotonin

Attachment = Oxytocin and Vasopressin

The above is the elementary roadmap to falling in love. In a world dominated by sources of feel-good dopamine, it is tough to get to a long-term attachment with a romantic partner.

Oxytocin is commonly known as the cuddle or bonding hormone. It feels great, but it's not quite as exciting as dopamine. Dopamine is a rollercoaster jam-packed with highs, lows, and loopy loops. It's exciting, dangerous, intoxicating, and addictive. Oxytocin is your affection for your grandparents or someone you've been friends with for 20 years. Their novelty has long worn off; it's safe and predictable. Why settle for safety and predictability when novelty and excitement are renewed with dopamine?

"We experience surges of dopamine for our virtues *and* our vices. In fact, the dopamine pathway is particularly well-studied regarding addiction. The same regions lighting up when we're feeling attraction light up when drug addicts take cocaine and when we binge eat sweets. For example, cocaine maintains dopamine signalling for much longer than usual, leading to a temporary "high". In a way, attraction is much like an addiction to another human being."[5]

People who fall victim to Disney are addicted to falling in love. We have a make-believe narrative trying to interpret biology, and it's a cluster fuck! As outlined earlier, you can only fall in love for the first time with that person once. Enjoy that feeling whilst it lasts because, like a drug addict chasing their very first high, you will never reach that high again with that person.

Dumpers and dumpees alike need to update their expectations of love. Seriously. It would be best if you made oxytocin your best friend. Otherwise, you will be on the Disney merry-go-round of lust, attraction, losing the spark, and breakups. Disney has, quite expertly, tapped into human biology with its ideologies and narratives.

This tumour has been growing for over a century. And now it must be removed because it's terminal to your relationships.

LOVE IS A CHOICE, NOT A FEELING

I feel like an imposter writing this part of the book. However, I can tell you that you must know that a relationship can end anytime, by anyone, for any reason. If you manage to reach the end, death will take that relationship. Sticking it out for the long-haul means accepting and embracing that all things end. Not only will it end, but there will be phases of boredom, loss, and sadness. But without these, we cannot know what happiness and excitement is. Embracing the unpredictability, strangely, gives you stability. You are likelier to do extra work without having the Disney feels.

Long-lasting love is a choice after the Disney feelings wear off. We only have a limited number of times to get it right. How many more times do you want to break up, start again, get the Disney feeling, lose the spark and break up again? Take it from me: I am now closer to 40 than 30, and as exciting as a new relationship can be, I certainly want to avoid being on the dating scene in my mid-40s or early 50s.

Past a certain point, we must choose to stay with our partner after the novelty has worn off. We must choose to perform maintenance and work on the relationship. We must perform maintenance and work on ourselves constantly. We must learn from every breakup and see it as training to get it right the next time.

How? Accept lessons taught by our ex-partners. This means giving your ex the breakup, giving them your silence, and accepting the gift of education. Doing so will help prevent future breakups because they taught you precisely the lessons you need to learn. The novelty of a new relationship is great, but it cannot sustain a relationship in the long haul. There shouldn't be any secrets to sticking it out for the long haul.

All you need to do is to change your idea of love:

- Swap **falling** in love for **choosing** to be in love
- Swap: "What can my partner do for **me**?" to "What can **I** do for my partner?"
- Swap the concept of the one for, "There are 40 million other matches out there!"
- Swap listening to **respond** for listening to **understand**
- Swap 'Me vs You' for 'Us vs the Problem'

Changing your mindset and habits regarding love can be the difference between sustainable long-term happiness and reading a book like this. Statistics show that in the U.S. 50% of 1st marriages end in divorce, 67% of 2nd marriages, and 73% of 3rd marriages.[6]

The Scribbler survey found that of all UK adults who are currently married:

- 84% of people who are married in the UK describe themselves as being "happily married"
- 8.2% say their marriage is "neither happy nor unhappy"
- And a further 8% say they're "unhappily married"
- 23.8% plan to divorce

It's quite scary to say that only, on average, three out of ten marriages are happy and successful.[7] And if only three out of ten marriages are happy and successful, then we are doing something very wrong to be fucking it up so badly.

If someone told you that you had a 70% chance of being shot every time you left your house, you wouldn't step out of your front door. One would hope you'd take better precautions, like wearing weapons-grade body armour or moving to a different area. So why not apply that to relationships and marriage by taking better precautions?

A great precaution is learning how to fight in a relationship. This can go a long way when preventing breakups. Sadly, couples are learning to fight while they are fighting. By this time, it is already too late. A typical example of fighting poorly is when clients tell me she always wanted more space, and he always wanted more closeness. One feels smothered, and the other feels abandoned. When the one who feels abandoned intends to reaffirm the connection, the smothered feels like their independence is threatened.

In every relationship, there is a pursuer and a distancer. Most people find this to be odd, but it's quite normal. Sadly, rather than discussing each other's needs and finding a compromise, the distancer tells the pursuer to chill the fuck out, and the pursuer tells the distancer they don't care about the relationship because they're not matching effort. The secret sauce to fighting well is to validate your partner's needs. You're not required to understand them; rather, be good at compromising.

The art of a good compromise isn't trying to keep everyone happy but ensuring no one is miserable. Can you give your partner that twenty-minute phone call that will mean the world to them? You probably could. Can you leave your partner alone for one day and not blow their phone up to give them the space they so badly crave? You probably could. Can you fight without screaming, shouting, bad language, or shutting each other down? Is simple communication all you really need? You probably could, as long as both parties unfuck themselves and listen to understand. It would be best to learn this before the fight occurs.

No one in their right mind would step into a boxing ring with a professional fighter to learn how to box. You learn how to box before stepping into the ring. You learn how to argue before stepping into the ring with your partner. Fighting is unavoidable. The person you love and marry is the person you fight with, so you must learn how to fucking fight in a way that will resolve the issue. Sadly, most people fight in a way that creates more fights in the future.

No one listens to understand and everyone points the finger at everyone else.

Exercise:

The next time you're in an argument with your partner: sit down, shut up and do nothing but listen. Can you listen to them without getting defensive? Can you say, "I hear you. Tell me more." Can you say: "That sounds frustrating. I am sorry what happened made you feel that way. What can I do to help us move past this? This is an Us vs the Problem. Not Me vs You."

Why wait until things get bad to make the changes? It's no different than your doctor telling you that if you stop smoking now, you'll live a long, healthy life. A lot of people will ignore the warning and stop smoking *after* they have been given a terminal diagnosis and then start performing maintenance.

By then, it's too late.

Why must it take you two, three, or four breakups before you realise it is you who must change? Why must it take your partner threatening to dump you? Why must it take your partner dumping you before you promise to do the maintenance required to keep the relationship alive?

Most people perform better maintenance on their cars than they do their relationships, and that's really fucking sad. An ounce of prevention is worth a pound of cure. Doing the tedious preventative maintenance and having awkward conversations will give you long-term happiness. It's not as exciting as what Disney sells you, but it will last longer.

Relationships are only as complex as you make them. If you want to avoid future breakups, learn your ex's lessons, do the self-work, and stop blaming the world and your ex for how you feel. There is a word for blaming your ex for everything:

Neediness!

Neediness is at the core of every Disney romance story because no one takes responsibility for their feelings and then employs the prince or princess to take away all their pain.

THE STORY OF TINDERELLA

I once worked with a young man, let's call him Link. Link isn't his real name, but to protect his identity and reference my favourite video game of all time, I will call him Link.

Link, known as Tinderella, got his nickname because he always had a funny date story. He would walk into the office most mornings, sharing tales of his date the night before. He was looking for "the one". He romanticised romance, and his Disney script gave him unrealistic expectations of love and relationships. According to him, there was always something wrong with the women he dated. All the women he dated were too fat, too skinny, not well educated, wear the wrong makeup, too blonde, too dark, breasts not big enough, and you get the picture. He was about as deep as a puddle and had a high-novelty drive. He would complain about being lonely and, in the same sentence, go on about how there were no good women out there.

There are plenty of good women; it's just he'd been fucked by the Disney ideology and impossible standards that he ended up single. His expectations were nothing more than an overcompensation for his neediness and low self-esteem.

Link had a Ferrari attitude. The only issue is that he had Toyota money. He was frequently overdrawn, overspending on first dates, buying designer brands, and renting a flat he could barely afford. He frequently complained he had no money; at one point, some of our mutual colleagues brought him lunch. He was convinced all women sought out men with a lavish lifestyle and, therefore, was always trying to be something he was not. If he did manage to impress a woman with his glamour, they quickly realised he couldn't sustain it and dumped his ass. Link obsessed over these women, constantly texting them on WhatsApp, love-bombing, and begging to see them. It was hard to watch, in all honesty, and we just felt bad for him. He would reject the women who were genuinely into him because they all had something wrong with them.

I shit you not, he rejected one woman because she started a PhD but didn't finish.

Pretty rich from a bloke who went from working in kitchens to sitting in an office job and spending every spare second he had harassing women way out of his league.

After a year of rejecting perfectly suitable women and being rejected by women who saw through his bullshit, he started to change. Sadly, not for the better. The only women left for him to date were those available to him: The crazies!

One morning, he glided into the office, as high as a kite on dopamine, because he met the one. He met a woman who shared the same love of classical music, which wasn't bad, but that was all they shared. No feeling-out process, no dating, and no screening. They moved in together within the month. He jumped into bed with a direct reflection of him—a self-entitled dopamine junkie with a high novelty drive and unrealistic expectations. Bonding over a love of classical music and narcissistic Disney scripts, they were perfect for each other.

For three months!

After three months of living together, the novelty wore off. But Tinderella was barred from the ball. When unrealistic expectations bond you and you only have one thing in common, happily ever after is a clusterfuck of narcissistic ideology. Unrealistic expectations of romance and relationships facilitated their expectations of each other. It wasn't the girl he liked; rather, it was the idea he built of her in his head. At this point, he was so desperate for a girlfriend that he went from being too picky, to not picky enough.

> "Today, we turn to one person to provide what an entire village once did: a sense of grounding, meaning, and continuity. At the same time, we expect our committed relationships to be romantic as well as emotionally and sexually fulfilling. Is it any wonder that so many relationships crumble under the weight of it all?"
>
> — *Esther Perel, Mating in Captivity*

Once the honeymoon was over, all Tinderella had left was a diminishing physical attraction, which was not enough. They booked one-way tickets to a breakup because what they bought into was too good to be true.

Link moved out after a messy breakup and was straight back on Tinder, looking for his next high. The following months were a string of funny but sad dating stories, as Link was no closer to unfucking himself and his delusional idea of love. He used the novelty of Tinder and a new woman daily to cure his loneliness and soothe his heartbreak rather than spending time working on himself. Link never found a way to break up with his breakup. Link never changed his Disney script. Link kept his Ferrari attitude whilst surviving on Toyota money. Link thought the rest of the world was crazy, and he was the sane one.

You know who else thought they were the sane one and the rest of the world was crazy? Adolf Hitler (more on him later).

Link flew through many women until he finally found himself in a relationship with a woman who was excessively emasculating. She dominated all areas of his life. I suppose this was inevitable as he had poor self-esteem. Link never loved himself enough so when someone came along offering this love, he was high as a motherfucker on feel-good neurotransmitters. That was the most loved he had ever felt. This new woman told him what to wear and who to hang out with. She berated him for indulging in his hobbies and would withhold sex from him if he didn't comply with her dictatorship. Do you know which other woman in Link's life treated him so cruelly? His mother.

Link was haunted by a dysfunctional mother-son dynamic. These toxic interactions from childhood had long-lasting effects on Link.[8] Co-dependency, low self-esteem, and emotional immaturity gives you Tinderella. He was an idealistic, lovesick puppy, outsourcing love, and validation from women because he never learnt how to give it to himself. He never learnt how to break up with his breakups, do the work on himself, and level up. He eventually found what he was looking for.

If Link were one of my breakup recovery clients, I would encourage him to delete the dating apps, stay single for a whole year, and focus on his relationship with himself. When we continuously outsource our emotional validation to a romantic partner, we're avoiding the pain and the opportunity to work on ourselves.

We're essentially taking an emotional painkiller. Ironically, the relief and happiness we seek are in the pain we're so desperately trying to avoid.

Take home points:

There is a difference between falling in love and being in love. After the Disney feelings have worn off, being in love is a conscious choice which requires ongoing effort and maintenance. How you feel in the 1st year compared to the 10th year will be vastly different.

Disney has you believing that happily ever after is a string of constant dopamine highs and that you'll fall in love forever.

Real, long-lasting love is boring and mundane. Learn how to do the boring well. Change your idea of love! Change what the one means. The one doesn't have to be your rescuer or the person who takes your pain away. The one can simply be a person that is a good balance for you. Your strengths will offset their weaknesses, and their strengths will offset your weaknesses. You both understand the need for safety in each other's company, adventure in each other's absence, and examination in exploring a growth mindset together.

Consider you and your partner like a Venn diagram. Remember those? I thought I would leave school and never think of a fucking Venn diagram again. Your circle is you and your independence. Your partner has their own circle. Then that area in the middle where you overlap, that's the part of your lives which intertwines or allows space for dependency.

Independence can vary, and so can dependency. Say your partner is normally financially independent, that's in their circle. Then they lose their job and have to ask you for help, that means you both put that into the shared space.

If you feel as if you're relying on your partner too much, you might change other parts in and out or expand and shrink the circle. For example, your partner isn't working, so they add cooking to their circle, thus gaining some independence and giving you both some room for dependency as you would be occupied with more financial responsibility.

Honestly, it's all about what you consider independence and what your partner considers it to be. What do you like to take care of? What does your partner like to take care of? What are your hobbies alone? What are their interests?

So unfuck yourself, do the self-work, and screen potential partners better. Your breakups are the perfect time to do this because relationships and breakups are separate entities which offer their own lessons.

What lessons did your ex teach you? Get a pen and paper and write this down.

After all, your ex will go from your biggest fan to the harshest critic so listen to them. Don't take it personally, merely as an opportunity to improve and get it right next time. Did they show you that you were overly anxious or avoidant? Were you listening to respond because you couldn't listen to understand? Did you even screen your ex correctly by asking the awkward questions during the dating phase? Such as:

- Have you ever cheated?
- If I were to call your ex, what would they tell me?
- What does a boundary look like to you?
- Are you able to respect other people's boundaries?

Nick's Law of Entitlement

You're entitled to love yourself unconditionally but not to unconditional love from a romantic partner. Romantic love is highly conditional, and the concept of the one is bullshit. The one is an ideology based on mythology. That shit will never outsmart biology, so don't try. You must constantly work on yourself. You do not want your partner to give you worth but to add to your own. You must then continue to work on yourself to maintain the relationship.

Real life is boring and that's okay. Happily ever after is doing the little monotonous things, well, every day. It is not a Disney feel-good adventure. Doing little things such as listening to understand and showing interest in your partner's interests and hobbies goes a long fucking way to ensuring the relationship is maintained. Showing up is maintaining healthy habits such as listening, learning, and working together where necessary. This also applies to a breakup because you will, especially, need to show up for the post-relationship with yourself.

Short-term gains provide long-term pain. You do not want to pursue continuous dopamine hits as they will make you miserable.

The unprecedented number of dopamine delivery systems we have today are short-circuiting our oxytocin, so we are insidiously good at normalising almost anything from your favourite foods to when you buy a new phone to starting a new relationship. It's never as good on day one thousand compared to day one when it was novel. Therefore, the more dopamine we get, the more we need to maintain our baseline. This leads people to seek novelty because nothing makes them happy continuously. If you're someone who must buy the latest iPhone, you're probably chasing highs and mistaking it for happiness.

Don't be a serial dater or dumper like our Tinderella (the bigger the highs, the bigger the lows). Link's unrealistic expectations of a potential new partner should show you two things:

1. The relationship with himself was practically non-existent and he hired one person to be his whole world and emotional validation. This was needy as fuck and too much for one person to bear. His neediness told everyone what they needed to know about him. He was not happy and he outsourced his entire happiness.

2. After failed dates due to unreasonable expectations and missing out on suitable matches, Link accepted defeat and settled for way below his worth and value.

Back to the conclusion.

The Disney fallacy is a societal problem contributing to unrealistic expectations about romance. And also even if you have a good heart, you might not find true love. But this doesn't mean accepting being treated like crap or emasculated but working with criticisms and issues to better yourself and your life. Only narcissists can't handle criticism, which leads them to become ignorant of their own flaws and shortcomings. Having a good heart isn't everything, either. You have to look after your health, mind, and body and pursue hobbies and interests.

The Disney ideology is especially harmful because it creates unrealistic expectations about what you can realistically expect in romantic relationships. Many struggle with feelings of inadequacy or low self-esteem, which unrealistic expectations can exacerbate. For example, people who are obsessed with the idea of the one or true love may believe that they are entitled to a beautiful, loving partner, regardless of their own flaws. This can lead to bitterness and resentment towards partners who do not meet their unrealistic expectations. These feelings can manifest in toxic and dangerous behaviours as, rather than focusing on themselves, they project their pain onto others.

The Disney ideology contributes to a cycle of unrealistic expectations and disappointment, damaging individuals and society further. It is important for you to understand that love and relationships are fucking complicated. So, focus on developing personal qualities such as empathy, communication, and emotional intelligence. You can join communities and support systems to develop skills and find personal fulfilment beyond a romantic relationship.

CHAPTER 3

Not So Magical Thinking

Consider trying to get your ex back like a drug addict going through withdrawal. The similarities are remarkable. People facing romantic addiction are often dependent on the high of falling in love as well as elements of hope, wishful thinking, and the thrill of the chase, which releases dopamine. In contrast, intimacy releases the bonding hormone oxytocin, and both are addictive to some. Withdrawal is the process of cutting out something addictive. In most cases, cutting back on addictive activities or alcohol or food and—in this case—your ex makes you realise how your very neurotransmitters have become dependent on their influence.

This is a very cold and clinical way to describe love but bear with me.

Spending significant time with a romantic partner leaves long-term changes. We grow used to their presence, altering our lives to spend time with them, subconsciously changing our dopamine, oxytocin levels, and other neurotransmitters. It is easy to become dependent. This is as dangerous as addiction. It is dependence.

Dependence is when we can no longer physically or psychologically function without that stimulus. When that addictive thing is gone, we manifest all sorts of physical and psychological symptoms. I've had clients tell me they can't eat, and when they do eat, they throw up. Some clients report headaches, muscle spasms, insomnia, diarrhoea, and even suicidal thoughts. If you have been experiencing similar symptoms, you should always speak to your doctor or mental health professional. I've certainly experienced extreme loss of appetite during breakups. When an ex-girlfriend of mine cheated on me in 2014, I lost 10kg (around 22lbs) in four weeks.

#breakupdiet

Depression, anxiety, mood swings, aches and pains, extreme fatigue, shaking, vomiting, and comfort eating can all happen. No wonder you want your ex back so badly. We become junkies.

And, like any junkie, we will do, say, or take anything to make the pain go away. For most, just hearing their ex-partner's voice can significantly ease these symptoms, but this is treating the symptoms and not the cause.

Drug addicts have one distinct advantage in many respects. They can take alternative safe substances to help wean them off their drug of choice. Most dumpees don't see the breakup coming and must deal with it cold turkey. However, doing so is itself a powerful drug of self-love. Not all drugs or junkies are equal, so choose your pain and choose the drug of self-love.

Let's get down to you with this cold and clinical explanation out of the way. Why do you *really* want your ex back so badly? Why are you, as well as so many others, willing to wait around for them?

Because you fucking love them and that's okay.

But it's more insidious than that; most people make their partners responsible for how they feel.

> "The second you make your partner responsible for how you feel, you remove your ability to control your life... I have one word for that! Disempowerment."
>
> Mark Manson, *Love Is Not Enough*

Before I go and get on my high horse again with what I am about to write, breakups fucking suck. I don't care how secure you are and how well-rounded your life is. It will hurt like a bitch.

Many of you may have a disorder of disempowerment. You've never taken the time to love and validate yourself, so you outsource to your partner. The problem is if they end the relationship, you, the dumpee, literally have nothing left. You made them your entire village. And the village left. They were your lover, best friend, carer, hobby, family, mentor, and therapist. Losing this is too much for anyone to handle. Getting them back feels like more than a want but a need because withdrawing from them is being left to sit in the pit of despair and self-loathing you dug years ago. All the love and support is just a bandage on that wound; once they take it away, the wound is exposed and festering.

WHY YOU SHOULDN'T GET BACK WITH YOUR EX

After my breakup, I spent much time imagining reconciling with my ex. I imagined the conversation, where we would have it, and how she would contact me. I imagined her name popping up on my phone, saying how much she missed me and wanted to make things work. I imagined meeting her on a warm, sunny day at our favourite restaurant. I imagined I would be wearing the new clothes I'd just bought because I chiselled 10lbs of fat off and looked good. Seriously, I was fucking smashing it in the gym, and I was walking around like I was sex on legs. I imagined her looking into my eyes and realising how stupid the whole breakup was.

My reconciliation fantasy never played out.

But, I began to realise how much work I had done for myself and my life. I'd drilled myself back into shape, paid a huge chunk of my mortgage, read more books in six months than I had in six years, I started playing the drums, going on adventures, meeting new people, reconnecting with friends and family, and I started my YouTube channel.

For the most part, I was doing well and felt somewhat okay. I asked myself, "What can my ex bring to the table if she comes back?" I started to realise there was a possibility that I'd levelled up to the point where she could no longer meet my minimum requirements for a partner.

I wondered: Should we ever take someone back who chose to walk away rather than work on things?

WHY YOU SHOULD NEVER TAKE YOUR EX BACK

Reason 1: You are worth more.

If they cheated, rebounded, monkey-branched, physically or mentally abused you, or were narcissistic... Do not *ever* take them back.

How someone treats you is a reflection of *them*.

How you *allow* yourself to be treated is a reflection of *you*.

If you take your ex back under these circumstances, you're projecting a complete disregard for your own autonomy, self-respect, and self-love. This means your ex can operate without consequence. You must practice self-worth, which means having strong and healthy boundaries for yourself. If your ex would constantly verbally abuse you, a strong boundary would be, "I will no longer tolerate verbal abuse from you. If you continue to abuse me verbally, I will walk away." Therefore, if you and your ex cannot agree to setting and respecting boundaries, know your worth and decline the reconciliation.

Disclaimer! If you were the abuser, cheater, toxic partner or narcissist, then your ex was right to leave you. If you were constantly accusing your ex of cheating, or protesting every time they spent time with someone you were jealous of and saying words like: "It's not you I don't trust, it the people who want to take you away from me" that's manipulation! That's abusive behaviour.

Something I learned from an ex when I would say the same protesting bullshit, back when I was an insecure dickhead. She told me that whoever approaches me and asks me out, can want me all they want. Nothing is going to happen because they do not have my permission.

Translation: no one can fucking take anyone away from you. They either gave the other person permission or you pushed them in that direction with needy behaviour.

Either way, it was your ex that made the choice, which means they're no longer choosing you or the relationship they shared with you.

You need to have love for yourself to know what love you're worthy of. If your partner makes you feel inferior or unworthy, you will know they don't respect you in the way you deserve. If they cannot do this, wish them well with the bed they made because they must lie in it all alone.

Reason 2: You are not the same person.

As the dumpee, you're forced to face the breakup pain from day one. Pain can be your best teacher if you let it be. Pain isn't there to hurt you, rather it is there to alert you to problems to be fixed.

As I said in the introduction, a breakup is a terminal diagnosis that will give you a new life, if you allow it to. Ergo, you were forced to change, and hopefully for the better. This may give you a different perspective on your ex. This new version of you may not like your ex. This new version might not be compatible with your ex any longer.

As most dumpers do not see anything wrong with their decisions or how they acted, they very seldom adopt a growth mindset and remain the same person they were when they shared a romantic relationship with you. If that version of them reaches out to you, wish them well because they no longer match your new level of growth.

By chance you do reconcile, what caused the first breakup will likely cause another. If you work on yourself, you will understand you are not the same person anymore. And if you are different now, you will not return to a place in the past.

They thought dumping you would be the answer to all their issues. However, it's been some time, the money has run out, their friends aren't available much, the rebound, monkey branch, friends with benefits have failed, and now their Saturday night looks really lonely. They scroll their contact list, looking for someone to validate their time. They find your name and see some low-hanging fruit that'll give them an easy sugar rush.

Why is this?

Our natural survival instinct is to return to where we feel safe. Being single and the sole provider for yourself is new and unnatural. Of course, you want to retreat to safety. That is why staying single and working on yourself is not easy. It requires focus and strength. Real love requires self-work, self-reflection, and accountability. If levelling up were easy, everyone would do it. That's why honeymoon and Disney junkies are the epitome of laziness because they are addicted to instant gratification.

Perhaps they thought the grass was greener by dumping you. But here is the thing: the grass is greener where you water it. They could've suggested couples therapy, expressing their uncertainties or setting healthy boundaries to avoid a breakup. Yet they took the easy way out and now want you back.

Don't ever be the back-up option. Don't be on their list if you're not first.

Reason 3: You or your ex resist learning crucial lessons.

They will probably leave you again, and the second time will be worse.

What lesson did your ex teach you?

What did they teach you about them?

What did they teach you about yourself?

I truly believe every ex teaches us the lessons we need to learn. For me, my ex dumping me taught me how a lack of boundaries and being too nice could be catastrophic to a relationship. It was easy to blame my ex for having an avoidant attachment style, but that was *her* burden. My burden was to understand my bullshit and improve in those areas. My burden was that it was me who chose her. I chose to lay with her, and I chose not to hold boundaries or communicate effectively what I wanted and needed.

Assuming you learn your lesson and gain the wisdom from it, did your ex do the same? Let's imagine they come back. The day you've been waiting for has arrived and your ex wants to meet you. You go for coffee. You're showing off your new, leaner body, sporting new clothes and you've worked on rewiring your mindset, to take responsibility for your contributions in everything you do. However, your ex hasn't changed even 1%. They blame you for everything and put unreasonable demands on you. They were the same demands they had of you from your shared romantic relationship, only this time you've learnt the magic that is having boundaries.

For the first time in your life, you say "No". Your anxiety goes up because saying that may cause your ex to abandon any attempts of reconciliation. But you know the last relationship failed because you had no boundaries, and you don't want to go back to that. Your ex protests and says, "You're being unreasonable!"

This is a deal breaker now.

You can either abandon the new you and give in to the unreasonable demands (which, and I promise you, will cause another breakup) or you can maintain your new, healthy boundaries and tell your ex to take it or leave it. If they don't respect your new boundaries then off they fuck. If they do respect your new boundaries, that may indicate they have also looked inward and learnt the lesson.

Either way, you will have your answer.

When they left you the first time, they set a precedent. You can tell more from someone's actions than someone's words. They are now a proven flight risk. And real love takes a lot of effort and hard work so when a honeymoon junkie chooses the path of least resistance and do whatever they can for their dopamine fix—they're lazy fuckheads! Why would you want to be with a fuckhead? Why would you take a fuckhead back?

I am saying fuckhead way too much now.

The same patterns and experiences repeat themselves because there is a lesson you need to learn. And you are resisting it! The same things keep happening and getting more difficult to handle until you recognise and eliminate the behaviour that needs changing.

If you thought the breakup felt terrible the first time, my friends, you will experience more pain than ever before the second time. It's just not worth it.

If they dumped you once, they would likely dump you again. Judge your ex by their actions, not their empty promises born out of the fear of being alone.

The first thing to do when you see the same type of event happening over and over again is ask yourself how you are feeling and why you are feeling that way:

- "I am afraid of being single forever."
- "I am so fucking angry they don't want to be with me."
- "I am so fucking upset they left me."
- "I am jealous they'll end up with someone else."
- "They're so fucking weird for not thinking the same as me."

Once you recognise how you're behaving, try to understand what has happened in your life to make you think this behaviour is necessary. Sometimes, it is tough to pinpoint but you bought my book so you're getting there!

Try to approach your thoughts with a positive intention:

- "I have faith that my life will turn out how I need it to. I am enough."
- "It's a shame but they had to follow their own path in life."
- "I have an abundance of opportunities ahead of me."
- "It is nice they're following their own desires and wants in life even if they don't include me."
- "Everyone thinks and acts differently. They have their life, and I have my own."

Changing behaviour takes a long time, especially when you've been acting a certain way for so long. But a breakup is a lesson to help you learn. It's time to sit down and listen.

Reason 4: They were your only source of happiness.

Outsourcing love, validation, and worth harms your sense of self. It is also impossible for another person to achieve. You see, by being emotionally dependent on your partner, you are set up for misery. You will be disappointed and frustrated if they fail to make you happy. I'm not saying you shouldn't be happy and excited around your partner, but happiness only comes from inside you.

Do you only want a romantic partner to make you happy? Don't get me wrong, love and relationships can be great, but don't forget your happiness. Relying on someone else's happiness is easy, but you're just suppressing your own misery.

Use this time to analyse what makes you happy—you alone. But how do you find out what makes you happy? Try:

- Listing your core values (what values and ethics are important to you)
- What are your hobbies?
- Do you have any passions?
- Which friends can you spend time with?
- Are there family members you enjoy seeing?

Really focus on yourself. By doing so, you will level up and feel better than you do dwelling on your ex. But it takes a lot of hard work and alone time. Getting back with your ex in the state they left you in is an exercise in futility. All you will be doing is resurrecting the decomposing corpse that is your old relationship, desperately trying to breathe life back into it.

It is also a poor reflection of your ex if they take you back to the state they left you in because they are lonely and have convinced themselves everything will be okay. You will never get the best version of your ex, and they will never get the best version of you. You are just fuelling anxiety and desperation for external validation. A reconciliation will surely only succeed if a good degree of separation and self-work has been done on both sides.

Entitled thinking

When you are stuck, only actions will move you forward. I have found a disorder of action when coaching people through their breakups. There is a tendency to ask, "Why me?" when something bad happens, such as a breakup. This, at its very core, is a privileged and entitled mindset. It is deferring responsibility away from yourself, assuming that your pain is somehow special, and blaming others beyond your control.

But pain can be paralysing to other cognitive abilities such as self-reflection and self-assessment. The dumpee overanalyses how the dumper hurt them, and their brain is in a feedback loop of narcissistic rhetoric:

- "How could they hurt me?"
- "How fucking dare they leave me!"
- "They will never be happy without me."
- "They will never find someone like me."
- "They're obviously happy without me."
- "I meant nothing to them!"

Narcissistic much?

You're so paralysed by this entitled victim mindset that you're sitting indoors on a Friday night, combing their social media for any evidence of them dating someone new or a sign they are hurting as much as you are.

Let's be real here. Dumpees become hugely narcissistic, and I'm guilty as charged. What's the world record for the most Mark Manson quotes in one book? Answers on a postcard:

"The deeper the pain, the more helpless we feel against our problems, and the more entitlement we adopt to compensate for those problems. This entitlement plays out in one of two ways: I'm awesome and the rest of you all suck, so I deserve special treatment. I suck and the rest of you are all awesome, so I deserve special treatment."

– Mark Manson, *The Subtle Art of not Giving a Fuck*

Psychological experts observe that when people don't receive the external validation they believe they deserve, it can result in high levels of stress and hurt. This emotional pain can twist into narcissistic rage. This is also called a 'Narcissistic Collapse' and, according to Nicole Artz LMFT, this collapse appears when someone cannot maintain their confident image.[9]

Narcissism is caused by a constant need for validation, so when the collapse occurs, it can be triggered as a self-defence technique whereby the self-image and self-esteem are threatened. I'm delving into this because the human brain has more than proved itself to be the cause of more pain than it's worth, and there's nothing wrong with acknowledging your subconsciousness has activated a protective measure against hurt.

The next stop on the narcissism train is scouring the internet for confirmation bias. You're frantically searching YouTube for: "How to get my ex back" and "What is my ex thinking?" You're pretty much doing everything you can to avoid taking action because that would mean letting them go as well as the relationship you've formed with your breakup.

It's time to level up.

But how do you unfuck yourself and get unstuck?

It's not common for a narcissist to wonder if they're narcissistic, especially how to stop being a narcissist. If you're worried you're displaying traits of narcissism, it's likely there are other issues afoot. Usually, this is trauma. To address any trauma, always see a mental health professional, but to overcome narcissistic tendencies, take it one day at a time:

Accept that no one is perfect

Everyone is different, and everyone messes up. Just accept things as they are without the need to control them.

Know your worth

You have worth and value which are not reliant on perfection. Narcissism is usually associated with shame or worthlessness.

Forgive yourself

It's okay if you've set unreachable expectations. But think about why you set goals so high in the first place. Take responsibility for your limits and give yourself compassion for any missteps.

Identify your triggers

One way to heal is to understand what triggers you. Pay attention to when you feel angry or out of control. What was happening? What contributed? The answers are clues to understanding your emotions.

Take it one day at a time

You can't control every outcome for every situation. You will feel anxiety if you worry about what is going to happen tomorrow or next week. Take it one day at a time to reduce the urge to control everything.

Stop making everything about you

Listen to others. Focus on others. You must break the habit of everything happening to you because you're you, and the world revolves around you. There is no such thing as the most important person in the room. Everyone is made of the same stuff at the end of the day.

Start saying yes

Your life was previously too comfortable to say yes. Being too comfortable is what got you here, so you may as well go and get uncomfortable. Start doing shit and stop complaining that it's hard.

Learn to quit well

If you've been pouring years of yourself into something and you or the situation is not improving, then it's time to quit and try something new. This is what your ex did! It simply stopped working for them. So, take a leaf out of their book. Quit and try something new. Quit the relationship with your breakup and start a new relationship with you.

As a content creator, it's fucking hard to put out new content weekly, let alone daily. I frequently get stuck. I can't tell you how often I was stuck while writing this book. Most days, I wanted to fuck it off and walk away. I would curse the universe with: "Why me, you sadistic cunt bag?"

But as I wrote the ways to heal pain, I began to drop my self-entitlement. I know every content creator goes through the same shit. I just have to work on the fucking problem! So, instead of just sitting there staring at the screen, I wrote a bunch of shitty words. I went and listened to audiobooks and read books for inspiration. Then I came back and put these shitty words into something half-legible.

So, write your shitty words, especially when your imagination doesn't quite have the answer just yet. If you didn't catch on there, that's a metaphor for: It's okay not knowing how to write the next chapter of your life but start fucking writing it anyway. Don't be paralysed by the ending! You're not at the end yet. Get excited by writing a new chapter with endless possibilities, all because your ex said no to you.

You've been given the gift of freedom. Do not waste it!

Get unstuck and get unfucked!

RADICAL ACCEPTANCE

You feel crap, blame your ex for how you feel, preventing you from accepting your situation. Your brain wins a gold medal in mental gymnastics as it finds new and clever ways to blame your ex and, thus, keep you stuck in the breakup mud. Blaming your ex is non-acceptance. Is that even a word? I don't give a shit. You get my point!

When it rains, do you run from doorway to doorway, getting wet all the while? Or do you accept that it is raining and walk with dignity? In principle, accepting a breakup is no different. It's more painful than walking in the rain, yes, but just like you end up getting wet, you'll end up getting hurt. Might as well walk—walk away—with dignity.

> "The next step after we discard our expectations and accept what happens to us, after understanding that certain things - particularly hard things - are outside our control, is this: loving whatever happens to us and facing it with unfailing cheerfulness. It is the act of turning what we must do into what we get to do."
>
> — Ryan Holiday, *The Obstacle Is the Way*

Replace the expectation that you'll get back together or get over the breakup eventually and think you will heal, level up, and move on to better things. Holy fuck, you're alive! The sun rose this morning. You have food in your belly and a roof over your head. You're doing just fine. Anything beyond this is negotiable.

Take home points:

Like a junkie trying to score their next hit, a dumpee's desire to win their ex back is little more than getting a hit of your desired drug to stop the hurting. For junkies, it's a class A drug, for the dumpee, it's their ex. It's a very cold and clinical way to describe how bad you feel after a breakup but understanding that all types of withdrawal will take care of themselves if we stop taking the drug.

When the medicine becomes the disease, it's time to change the medicine.

Your new medicine is now no-contact, a commitment to self-love and self-validation. Constantly returning to the drug that made you sick will disempower you. The last thing anyone wants is their ex to have power over them.

There are a myriad of reasons not to get back with your ex. I have listed but a few here, but I encourage you to sit down with a pen and paper and write why your ex is wrong for you. Really let them have it and write down every shitty thing they did and said to you. This will help break the fantasy you have built up in your head. Most of the desire to get an ex back is fantasy. You only remember the good times.

Fuck that!

Remember the bad times and use that as fuel to catapult you to new adventures and people.

Write the next chapter of your life with shitty words. It's okay not to know your next step, or maybe you can't find the words. Write it anyway. Action, even shitty action, will help get you unstuck. I have been stuck writing this book for months at a time, but writing shitty words, just like what I am doing right now, moved everything forward.

You can edit later. Get the basics down and write chapters that don't involve your ex. You can say yes to new things and learn to quit well by quitting your breakup. Take extreme responsibility for everything. Responsibility releases you from the victim's mindset and moves you to the student's mindset.

CHAPTER 4

No Contact: The Story of Loving Yourself More Than Your Ex

What is no-contact? Before getting into this chapter, I want to be very clear on no-contact with an ex-partner. No-contact is when you have no form of contact with your ex-partner. No calls, no texts, and no emails. You unfollow them on social media. You reject all offers of friendship until you can be around each other without feeling weird.

Whilst I maintain that no-contact is the best way to help facilitate a reconciliation, it should never be weaponised to get your ex back. No-contact is for you to get you back. No-contact is a mindset. It is also a set of rules to live by to help get you through this horrid time. It's a mature reaction which takes strength post-breakup. You respect the dumper's decision as well as the consequences. Do not make yourself available to them.

Go no-contact.

INCORRECT INTENTIONS

I was doing no-contact wrong. I had consumed a ton of breakup content. I obsessively thought: "One more day of no-contact and she'll reach out." This thought sustained me for a long time. But, just like only eating salads on a diet, my appetite left me dissatisfied and unfulfilled. At my lowest points, typically on Friday and Saturday nights, I wrote out needy text messages begging my ex to reconsider us. My finger would hover over the 'send' button, but I never pulled the trigger. It took every fibre of my being not to do it, and I was close more than once.

Some time passed when it finally hit me. She wasn't coming back. Her actions, or lack thereof, told me everything I needed to know. She didn't want me. I really thought no-contact would build the want and regret in her, but it never did. She never came back. I fell into a dark slump and tried dating between COVID-19 lockdowns, but I couldn't quite see the light. I know now that I could've been healing during the no-contact period rather than wishing for them to change their mind.

Although no-contact can offer the best possibility for an ex to come back, that should never be a primary motivation. No-contact is to get you back! It is for healing. When I started to apply that mindset, I flourished. I wasn't over her by any means, but I started to choose to love myself more than my ex.

No-contact is like eating your veggies. It sucks at first. You don't appreciate their health benefits and would rather eat a pizza. Or, in the case of a breakup, you'd much rather be strategising the return of your ex. If getting abs results from all the pizza you didn't eat, then no-contact results from resisting the urge to reach out to your ex. For me, it paid off massively in the end. But hours felt like days, and I felt stuck for the longest time.

Just like going to the gym, the reps compounded over time. Every day, each rep makes you stronger. Lifting weights until your muscles are swimming in battery acid is not fun. You may be stuck lifting the same weights for a while, but one day, doing the shit you hate to do like you love it pays off. No-contact compounds are the exact same. It makes you stronger. A little doesn't look like a lot but do it daily, and you'll start seeing results. But I know the physical and mental benefits of consistently pushing yourself a little more every day. You'll hate to be in this much discomfort but do it like you love it. No-contact is no different.

NO-CONTACT IS THE ART OF DOING NOTHING!

On October 7th, 2008, Qantas flight Seven Two was on a routine five-hour flight between Singapore and Perth, Australia. Onboard the Airbus A330, one of the world's most modern, advanced, and safest passenger jets, were 303 passengers and 12 flight crew. It was a sunny day with mild winds and low air traffic. Conditions were perfect for a smooth and uneventful flight.

In command was Captain Kevin Sullivan. He was a former TOPGUN Fighter Pilot flying for Qantas since 1986. In terms of experience, you would be hard-pressed to find someone with as much airtime as Captain Sullivan. Qantas is also considered the world's safest airline, so you can't hope for a safer environment when you combine the flight crew's experience with the airline's safety record.

The flight crew configured the A330 for take-off, taxied to the runway, and engaged the take-off thrust to get 242 tonnes of commercial jet into the air. Thirty minutes into the flight, the master caution light came on, alerting the flight crew to a potential issue with the plane. The flight computer displayed the error: 'Air engine bleed 1 fault' (bleed air is air siphoned off from the engines to pressurise the cabin).

 Let's say you won't have a safe and enjoyable flight without pressurisation in an aeroplane.

The crew quickly corrected the error, and everything on the flight deck returned to standard operations. However, these were the force readings from the flight computer snowballing into a cluster of problems, putting the plane and its passengers in mortal danger.

At 12.35pm Perth time, the A330 was approaching the northern coast of Australia when the autopilot disconnected without warning. Captain Sullivan, without hesitation, immediately grabbed the sidestick and took control of the plane whilst the co-pilot set about diagnosing the issue. They switched to the backup autopilot to stabilise the plane. But to their surprise, the flight computer displayed a litany of faults and downing systems. To put it mildly, they were confused as fuck because such a thing was not meant to be happening on a modern jet. Suddenly, the plane called out a warning no pilot wants to hear: "Stall, stall, stall." The stall warning alerts the pilots that they were about to fall out of the sky because the plane wasn't flying fast enough to maintain the pressure differential over the wings to keep them in the air.

The pilots were confused and had no idea what was going on. It was a clear day, so they could see the plane was level, and the flight instruments confirmed that the A330 was flying at the correct speed. Then, the master alarm in the cockpit began to sound. The flight computer reported new faults, while the captain's speed and altitude instruments flashed conflicting readings. The plane was simultaneously telling the captain that they were flying too slow and about to stall whilst blaring an over-speed warning, telling them the plane was flying faster than it was designed to.

The readings were impossible and didn't make any sense.

The captain looked at his backup instruments and those of the co-pilots. Both sets of readouts were the same, and the captain determined that his flight instruments were faulty and, therefore, unreliable. Therefore, he focused on the backup instruments whilst using the co-pilot instruments to confirm that what he saw on the backup was accurate.

The passengers were unaware of what was going on in the cockpit. Despite the faults on the plane, it was still functional enough to maintain normal flight until it wasn't! You need to know that Airbus airplanes have incredibly sophisticated computers and automation to assist pilots. They have supremely robust safety mechanisms in place. For example, if it detects a stall warning and the pilot does not act, the safety systems will push the nose down and increase engine power to restore the airspeed to a safe point, keeping the plane in the air.

And that was exactly what happened. Only the plane was not in danger of stalling. It turned out the flight computer CPU malfunctioned, and they believed the plane's nose was too high and was about to stall the aircraft. The safety systems kicked in violently, pushing the nose towards the Indian Ocean.

The A330 was nosediving towards the sea at 800kph (almost 500mph). Those in the back who weren't wearing seatbelts were slammed into the bulkheads as the plane entered zero gravity.

Captain Sullivan pulled on the sidestick to stabilise the plane, but nothing happened. The plane believed it was in danger and it was ignoring the commands of its human masters. The harder the captain pulled back on the sidestick, the more the plane resisted, doing the exact opposite. Captain Sullivan, with his vast wealth of knowledge in aviation, remembered something from his fighter jet days. The planes he flew then were less sophisticated than the A330, but the principles of aviation remained largely the same.

He did the most counter-intuitive thing most people would've done in this situation. He did nothing! More to the point, he stopped fighting the plane and released the controls for a few moments as he realised he could be making the situation worse. Pulling back aggressively on the sidestick could've caused the aircraft to pull violently upward, causing an actual stall. After those precious few seconds of doing nothing, Captain Sullivan pivoted to a gentler approach, stabilising the plane.

As gravity returned to normal, those pinned to the bulkhead slammed back down to the floor, causing severe injuries. The crew managed to make a successful emergency landing, and everyone survived.

So how the fuck does this story help you get over a breakup?

Just like the title of this book, it is a counter-intuitive remedy for heartbreak! It was the counter-intuitiveness of Captain Sullivan that saved the plane. He paused, accepted the situation, and did the only thing he could do at the time. Nothing! Those crucial few seconds of letting go allowed everything to reset, and rather than trying to force the plane back to normal, he applied the bare minimum force. He realised that brute forcing the situation was likely to cause further issues.

When the medicine becomes the disease, one must change the medicine.

The thing most breakups and probably yours have in common is that people try to make something happen. Force creates resistance, and therefore, the more you do, the more you force it, the worse you make the situation, causing your ex to nosedive even faster and further away from you. No-contact is merely the mechanism you use to achieve your recovery. No-contact is the art of doing nothing for a few moments to choose a better course of action.

Why must you go no-contact? Look at it this way. What other fucking choice do you have? No-contact is a story of loving yourself more than you loved your ex or wanting to get them back. It is self-parenting. It is deferring gratification. It is sacrificing your medium-term urges so you can achieve your long-term goals. In the dumpee's case, the long-term goal should be to get themselves back, which might offer the best possibility to facilitate a reconciliation.

No-contact is the only real response to being dumped. Your first reaction might be to do everything you can to convince your ex to come back to you, but you cannot out-logic feelings. Think of a time when you made up your mind about something. Could anyone talk you out of it, no matter how logical their argument was? They may have even tried to talk you out of dating your ex, but you felt the spark, right? Your ex does not want to be reasoned with immediately post-breakup. They have spent a significant amount of time and emotional resources figuring out how to dump you. They're in relief, and you must let them have it.

Exercise:

Think of when you were putting off having a difficult conversation with someone. Do you remember the mental gymnastics, anxiety, and imaginary conversations you had beforehand? The build-up is torture. Now, focus on the relief you felt after you got what you needed to say off your chest. Maybe it wasn't your ideal outcome, but nonetheless, you're no longer stuck in the mud.

That is where your ex is after the breakup conversation. They feel free of the mud your relationship was in and need to be allowed to explore the relief it provides. Begging, pleading, nagging and trying to out-logic their feelings is possibly the least attractive thing you can do. It shows desperation, validates their decision to leave and reinforces their belief that you do not listen to or understand them. However, if you agree with them, back off, and give them the space they crave, they will feel listened to and understood. Your neediness will make you invisible to the person you most want to notice you.

> "It is possible to commit no mistakes and still lose. That is not a weakness. That is life."
>
> – Captain Jean-Luc Picard,
> *Star Trek: The Next Generation*

Yeah, I'm a Star Trek fan! Get over it!

I've said it a thousand times. Some exes just don't come back. You can do no-contact perfectly, and they may never reach out. Therefore, I always urge you to assume your ex will never come back. Going no-contact can feel extreme. It's natural to be hesitant. But in most situations, it's important after a breakup. You must choose when to do nothing and when to do something.

In my experience, most people who want their ex back should go no-contact to make them stronger. Those who actually *need* to implement no-contact are usually most resilient towards it. No-contact is giving yourself control of the things you can control. You can only control how you think, feel, and respond.

So fuck what your ex is doing, thinking, or saying!

Accepting your ex's decision to leave your relationship. This is the first step. The second is responding to your feelings. So maybe you did everything right and still lost. You cannot do anything, but you can choose how you move on from that failure.

UNORTHODOX NO CONTACT

Student or victim. Abundance mindset or scarcity mindset. Choose your path very carefully because one has a great future, and the other does not. If you want a reconciliation, you must be better than the person your ex left. Sitting around and licking your wounds for too long attracts other wounded animals. Will your ex want to be around wounded animals? Probably not. And if they don't come back, then who gives a fuck? You got *you* back and moved on to bigger and better things!

There is no downside to going no-contact. Let no-contact be the opportunity that you need to heal and improve. So, let's ensure you get it right.

Let's call these tips Nick's Five Unorthodox No-Contact Tips. Ten points for originality, again! Here are five unorthodox ways to turbocharge no-contact:

Nick's Five Unorthodox No-Contact Tips

1. Give yourself time to feel bad

Feel it to heal it. There is a time and a place to feel shit. So, feel sorry for yourself and play the victim. Yes, you heard that right. Spend a week or so in bed, watching Netflix and eating the full-fat ice cream. Get it out of your system because there is much work to do. Play the victim for a little bit because it will make you realise how shit being a victim is. Say to yourself, "How fucking dare they break up with me? Me!" Or, "How could they hurt me so badly?" Write a shit list on your ex. List all the shitty things your ex said and did. Let them have it. Then, write a second list describing what your ideal partner would be like. Compare the two lists. Why would you want your ex when they're nothing like your ideal partner?

> "Choose not to be harmed—and you won't feel harmed. Don't feel harmed—and you haven't been."
>
> — Marcus Aurelius, *Meditations*

When we are in pain, it's sometimes hard to accept that there's nothing we can do to change things. We often think of sadness and longing when we think about a breakup. This pain can be very intense and come in waves over many weeks or months. Pain comes in waves, and it can feel like nothing will ever be right again. But gradually, most find the pain eases, and it is possible to accept what has happened. Once you've done feeling sorry for yourself, choose not to be harmed any longer.

2. No-contact with your ex is the perfect time to get shit done

Retreat inward to enrich your soul with experiences you need and hobbies you want to pursue. Take time to find your purpose.

That trip with your friends you've been putting off? Book it! That renovation in your house you've been putting off? Start work on it! That hobby you stopped doing? Start it up! Get intentional and find a new you.

> "Nowhere can a man find a quieter or more untroubled retreat than in his own soul."
>
> – Marcus Aurelius, *Meditations*

By finding your purpose, I promise you this: you will add meaning to your life. If you haven't spent much time thinking about your purpose, you might have preconceived ideas about what it could be. But these types of achievements often don't bring the fulfilment that comes with finding your personal sense of purpose.

Your purpose is your why.

This sense of purpose guides and sustains you. Day to day and through the years. Even when you have setbacks, and the world turns upside down, purpose gives you stability and a sense of direction. Finding purpose is essential for living a happy, healthy life.

People who have a purpose do not worry about things beyond their control—lions do not concern themselves with the opinions of sheep. You can either be the author of your story or just the observer. Choose wisely.

3. Stop counting the days

No-contact can become a bad habit for many people because they count the days since the breakup. These types of people weaponise this and become obsessed to the point they're in a relationship with the breakup. They wait for their ex to reach out again rather than move on.

You must stop counting the days. If you're saying to yourself something like: "40 days no-contact", "41 days no-contact", and "It's been 50 days no-contact, so they're bound to text me now"; your intention with no-contact is all wrong.

Change the intention to: "I will not contact my ex so I can heal and get myself back." If you like counting so much, count your calories and steps. You'll look better, feel better, and you'll look banging in the new clothes you'll need to buy because of how sexy you now look. Just imagine the look on your ex's face if they were to see you in the street.

> "You do not rise to the level of your goals, you fall to the level of your systems."
>
> — James Clear, *Atomic Habits*

4. Change the story you're telling yourself

I hear the following every day without fail: "My ex moved on so quickly with their rebound. No doubt they are happier without me!"

Err no! See things for what they are.

In most cases, rebounding or dating too soon isn't moving on. It's outsourcing the grief of a breakup from another. From your perspective, it looks like your ex and their new partner have "the spark" or whatever the fuck that means! That spark really is this: two people putting on a performance. That mask will slip eventually, and the value (or lack thereof) will be exposed.

> "See things for what they are. Do what we can. Endure and bear what we must. What blocked the path now is a path. What once impeded action advances action. The Obstacle is the Way."
>
> — Ryan Holiday, *The Obstacle is the Way*

Remember, your ex had to go through pain to end a relationship with you. They must grieve as well. But this process usually starts before they break up with you. Therefore, fuck what you see on social media, and fuck what your imagination is telling you. Just do the best you can.

Rebounds or social media posts are breadcrumbs! So, stop baking narratives out of them. Think about why you're trying to anyway. Your past trauma and anxiety feed you false realities.

Repeat after me: "I have zero control over my ex. They're doing the best they can based on their trauma and experiences. I don't have time for that because I must use this time to get me back, and therefore, I will start digging my way out. Because if they do come back, I better ensure I've healed, grown, and am in-fucking-destructible."

Endure what you must, and what blocked the path has become the path.

5. If you tell yourself you can't do something, you're right

If you're telling yourself you can't do something, you're right; you can't. But if you flip it and tell yourself: "I can do this", you're also right; you can. You must be intentional with this shit. It is a conscious decision. I want you to say: "I can do this." You must be a willing participant in your rescue, and you must be your own cheerleader. Because, guys, no one can do this for you. No one can dig you out. Your friends and family can offer you help, and books like this can show you the door, but you're the one who must walk through it.

> "Whether you think you can, or you think you can't – you're right."
>
> – Henry Ford

The universe is nearly 14 billion years old. You popped into existence one day. If you're lucky, you will live for 70 to 100 years and then pop out of existence. The time you have to occupy the universe's canvas is like a drop in the ocean or a grain of sand on a beach. Do you have the time to waste on someone no longer invested in you? Probably not, and that is why no-contact must be for you and to get you back.

REASONS WHY YOUR EX MIGHT CONTACT YOU

It is important to understand that breakups are hard for many dumpers. Unless your ex is a sociopath, or has Narcissistic Personality Disorder, they will likely feel the breakup. This book isn't about vilifying the dumper (even though it does come across that way in some chapters) but understanding them as their own person with their own wants and desires rather than an extension of you. But, like I said in the introduction, I'm an uneducated fuckhead with too much time on his hands and a platform to voice my opinion. The truth is, dumpers hurt, too.

To be able to break up with your breakup, one must try to look at the breakup from the dumper's point-of-view. Their torment mostly happened pre-breakup. The dumpee's pain is exclusive to post-breakup. However, in many cases, the dumper has a secondary bout of pain, especially if the dumpee goes no-contact well. The dumper will remember their connection with you. They may reminisce over your funny little habits and how you made them laugh and feel. These things cannot be replicated by someone else because we never love two people the same way.

People get angry in the heat of the moment, but when the anger recedes, sobering thoughts begin to take over, anxiety spikes, and loneliness sets in. Our thumbs quickly start typing: "Hey, how are you?"

My first ever love was a fairy tale. She was the first girl I fell in love with. I lost my virginity when we were both young and very awkward. We were perfect for each other at this time in our lives. After we broke up, I never loved a girl quite the same. I fell in love again. Each time was different and unique, depending on the girl I was with and where we were in life. After the breakups, regardless of if it was me doing the dumping or being dumped, I didn't just stop loving them. Some of them reached out to reconcile. Other times, it was me reaching out.

The point is: we don't just *forget*.

Five reasons why your ex might contact you:

1. The exit strategy fails

This type of dumper will typically rebound, monkey branch, or cheat. If this is the case for you, fuck 'em off. Do not even entertain a response. They only reach out because their exit strategy failed. Their anxiety is high, and they reach out to their backup option—you. Seeing them again will give you the best dopamine high since the breakup. Hello dopamine, my old friend. Goodbye anxiety, I've been validated again.

Like a drug addict going through withdrawal, it's like being offered meth. Your ex is offering you a juicy stash of the purist Heisenberg meth. Or like curry to a pisshead (for non-UK readers, pisshead is British slang for someone who consumes copious amounts of alcohol, whereby curry is the food of choice).

Do not take what they're offering because they don't really want you. They want to soothe their anxiety. They will use you to get over you. A rebound avoids emotions and feelings in the previous relationship. Avoiding the pain of a breakup and the following uncertainty will make you feel much worse. You'll be back at the beginning of the healing process again. Do not allow your ex to delay your breakup process with your breakup.

2. Single life can suck balls for the dumper

I fucking love single life. In fact, it will take an exceptional woman to convince me not to be single. Being single means I can know who I really am and what I really need.

Most dumpers do not do the work, so they find single life to be overrated. However, when they finally dump you, they are thinking about how great it will be to have a metric fuck-ton of freedom. Even if they offer friendship, reject this and wish them well. So, you think being friends will make you happy, but it won't. It's an insidious novelty.

We are social creatures. We need a village of people around us. The dumper is trying to build a new village by maximising their newfound freedom. They hit the bars, clubs, go on a few trips that you never wanted to do because their trips are fucking stupid. And for a few weeks, it is all novel and new. However, your brain, being the fuckhead it is, normalises it. After the 10th straight weekend getting smashed or the 20th trip to the 20th country, it all becomes the same old same old.

Now, they look for the next distraction. The money is running out, and their friends are unavailable. No one is messaging them, they're comparing their real life to everyone else's fake bullshit on social media, and all of a sudden, absolute freedom means nothing without someone to share it with.

For the first weekend since the breakup, they sit in with Ben & Jerry's and Netflix, which, to be fair, sounds like a great weekend. They reach for their phone and open WhatsApp only to see how far you've slipped down the list. Then it hits them. You didn't even reach out to say, "I hope you're okay." You have no social media activity, so your imagination is left to fill in the gaps.

The euphoria of a single life wears off. They're just thinking about you.

3. They made a mistake

Maybe they never stopped loving you and needed time away from the relationship. Maybe they had a knee-jerk reaction and overreacted. Maybe they realised the grass is greener where you water it. Maybe they have to work just as hard as you to make it work.

If this is your ex, and you're both accountable and holding space for each other, I wholeheartedly encourage you to reconcile. Those who can take responsibility for their bullshit and how they respond to it are more likely to work with rather than against you.

Us vs the Problem! Not Me vs You! The caveat here is that the dumper must be the one to reach out. It was their idea to leave, and it must be their idea to come back.

4. You're the safety net

You've agreed to stay in contact, hoping you can show them how great you are. What really happened is the dumper has turned you into the emotional partner.

An emotional partner means they're fucking someone new who meets their physical needs while they're emotionally unavailable. They've contacted you for their emotional needs. You, the dumpee, manage all the non-physical and sexual sides of this new relationship.

They do this because you feel safe but not safe enough to be in a relationship with. They may even give you a sympathy fuck, but they still don't want you enough to reconcile.

5. They genuinely miss you

Your ex spent a lot of time with you. They may have seemed cold and heartless during the breakup, but like most other human beings, their feelings will catch up with them sooner or later. We all like to feel safe and like what is familiar. You both created fun, happy and cherished memories. This doesn't just vanish even when they decide to decouple from you. Dumpers are on a different journey to the dumpee, but their paths cross sooner or later. Dumpers hurt and have feelings, too. It is important to remember that.

WHAT TO DO IF YOUR EX CONTACTS YOU

There may come a time when your ex reaches out to you. It may be when you've been doing okay for a few months. You're still hurting, but you've been rebuilding your life only for them to throw the cat amongst the pigeons by contacting you, but you must stay in your centre. There is no point in doing all the work on yourself to revert to type just because your ex reached out. Your anxiety will probably go up 200%, but you must choose to respond with non-neediness and match their energy, assuming, of course, you want to reply. If you genuinely do not want to reply, by all means, fuck this part of the book off and move on.

Most of you will likely be counting the seconds until your ex reaches out and they finally have, so what should you do? Staying faithful to your recovery journey, you must take stock of everything leading up to the breakup. How did your ex handle the breakup, and did they rebound or cheat on you? If someone rebounds or cheats on me, they are never coming back. That's personal, but I must enforce my will upon you.

Regardless of your metrics and my god complex, step back and think about whether you want to re-engage with this person simply because your anxiety is high or because you feel there is a real chance. Anxiety can lure us into a false sense of fighting for something that maybe should've died a long time ago. Remember that no-contact's goal is to neutralise your ex's hold over your emotions. Therefore, if they were to reach out, they can very easily nullify your no-contact boundary, leading you into a false sense that they want me back, when in reality, their anxiety was just high, and they freaked out.

We should all try to be human and be kind to one another. You may be so angry that you want to scream, but if this book teaches you anything, it is the power of making better choices. Your ex did what they did and said what they said. You now have a wonderful opportunity to show them how you've grown by responding maturely and stoically. You must remember when your ex dumped you. That's how they felt at the time. They have had time to reconsider the relationship with you and have decided it's worth trying again.

Then again, their backup plan may have failed, and they are returning to you because it is safe and easy. This is why how the breakup was handled and what they did post-breakup should guide your actions.

Regardless of your response, you must remain in *your* centre.

Let's call this next part:

Nick's Guide for Responding To An Ex When In No Contact

10/10 for originality again. I know what you're thinking. How does he come up with this stuff?

1. Match their energy.
    Very simply, if they say: "Hey, how are you?" You match like for like: "Hey, I'm good, how are you?"

2. Give it some time before responding.
    An hour or two is fine. After all, you should be busy with other endeavours.

3. Do not discuss the relationship or breakup unless they do.

   Let them lead the conversation. It was their decision to leave, so let them make the decision to come back.

4. Go about your life.

   Too many slam the brakes on their hobbies, friends, family, and careers just because their ex reaches out. Go about your day like nothing out of the ordinary happened.

5. If they are with someone else, do not even entertain a conversation.

   You think you're in pain now? See how it feels when the person you want most in the world breadcrumbs you with false hope. In any case, you're not working on yourself to put up with such low-ball offers.

6. Enforce your boundaries.

   Ask them not to contact you any longer. This will hurt, but this is enforcing self-love. The pain is necessary because you're trying to get you back, not your ex. However, self-love is far less painful than clinging to false hope.

7. You must be objective.

   Did their Plan B fail? Are you now Plan C? If they rebounded, cheated, or monkey-branched after breaking up with you and failed, you're now the backup of the backup.

8. "I made a mistake. Let's meet."

   If all is going well and they made a genuine mistake breaking up with you due to other circumstances, then the offer of meeting up may not be one to reject. Consider whether they've rebounded and cheated or if they've been struggling since the breakup.

9. Be wary of bullshit.
Some words can be false narratives that lure you back: "I miss you. I love you. I can't stop thinking about you." Be mindful of: "I made a mistake. I choose you. I choose our relationship." If their reconciliation means less than nothing, then do not accept it, but if they're checking up on you as their priority, then perhaps it's not such a bad idea.

10. Practise self-preservation.
Protecting yourself is key. If seeing your ex will dismantle your emotional or psychological stability, then say: "Thank you for reaching out, but this does not work for me. Please only contact me if you want to reconcile because not having contact is for healing and moving on. You reaching out without the intention of reconciling is disrupting that process."

I fully appreciate your ex reaching out. It can take tremendous bravery but it can feel like all of your birthdays came at once, and thus you must be wary. Some things are too good to be true and if you're emotionally vulnerable, then you are more likely to accept your ex's return. For a short time, it will feel like euphoria. Their presence soothes all the pain you've endured. Yet, all the boundaries you've set will disappear when this happens. You've been handed the emotional painkiller, and you'll do almost anything to get more.

What do you do now?

Hold on to the pain. Do not allow your ex to soothe it. Reaching out doesn't necessarily mean reconciliation. Your ex may just be feeling lonely and only want validation. They either don't care or are not aware of the emotional ramifications.

So, what?

This can only happen if you allow it to happen. They can only affect you if you allow them to. It's all on you. It is your responsibility to examine them objectively.

Is this easy to do? Fuck no!

I am not saying you will feel great doing it. However, you must choose to respond in a way that serves you best, even if it means rejecting their texts and phone calls.

CHAPTER 5

The Common Denominator– It's You!

We all have baggage, but we mustn't let our baggage weigh us down. I've mentioned before I have been anxious as fuck most of my life. Childhood trauma, rejection, and a lack of self-love gave me a clusterfuck of insecure relationships.

I was hopelessly attracted to women with avoidant attachment styles or who needed a little fixing—the damsel in distress locked in a tower guarded by a fire-breathing dragon. I signed covert contracts with these women, because they had potential and they were a project I could work on. A covert contract is when we secretly say to ourselves, things like: "I will fix all your bullshit and you will fix all my bullshit because I'm anxious and insecure."

As someone who was anxiously attached to my partners, my history of long-term relationships history is fucked up.

But what do I mean by attachment style?

What does this have to do with you?

Psychologist John Bowlby was the first attachment theorist. He described attachment as a "lasting psychological connectedness between human beings."[10] Bowlby was interested in the anxiety and distress people experience when their emotional bonds are disrupted. According to psychologist Mary Ainsworth, the quality of the bonding you experience as a child determines how well you relate to other people and respond to intimacy.

If your primary caretaker made you feel safe as an infant, if they responded to your cries and understood your changing physical and emotional needs, you likely developed a successful, secure attachment. As an adult, this translates to being self-confident, trusting, and hopeful, able to healthily manage conflict, respond to intimacy, and navigate the highs and lows of romantic relationships.

If you experienced confusing, frightening, or inconsistent emotional communication as a child, though, if your caregiver was unable to comfort you or respond to your needs, you're likely to have experienced an **insecure** attachment. Infants with insecure attachment grow into adults who have difficulty understanding their own emotions and the feelings of others, limiting their ability to build or maintain stable relationships. They may find it difficult to connect with others, thus shy away from intimacy, or be too clingy, fearful, or anxious in a relationship.

Of course, experiences that occur between childhood and adulthood can impact and shape our relationships. Two people can experience the same trauma and develop very different attachment styles. However, the infant brain is so influenced by the attachment bonds that understanding your attachment style can offer vital clues as to why you may have relationship problems.

Perhaps you are self-destructive?

Maybe you make the same mistakes.

Do you struggle to form and stay in a relationship at all?

THERE ARE 4 MAIN TYPES OF ATTACHMENT STYLES:

Secure

Does what it says on the tin. The secure is typically a well-rounded individual, holding boundaries while communicating clearly and able to be vulnerable and intimate in a healthy way.

Avoidant

There are two types of avoidant: dismissive-avoidant and anxious-avoidant. The avoidant wants intimacy but it scares the shit out of them. At one time in their life, their needs weren't met, and they fear being hurt again.

Anxious

There are two anxious types: preoccupied and ambivalent. Much like the avoidant, the anxious needs were not met. The anxious attachment has a counter-strategy to the avoidant. They demand an unsustainable level of security. The second they feel unsafe or unwanted, they are triggered. It's like a bad day in Chernobyl.

Fearful Avoidant

This is like a super-hybrid of the avoidant and the anxious all in one. Avoidant + anxious = you won't know what fucking day it is when dating someone with a fearful avoidant attachment style. They likely have the deepest wounds and need the most help to validate the fearful-avoidant. So, if you find yourself dating a fearful avoidant, you can show understanding and compassion, but it may not be the right time for a relationship with that person.

THE RELATIONSHIP HISTORY OF AN ANXIOUS MAN (ME):

My first love

I was an extreme-anxious, and she was an extreme-avoidant. The closer I needed to feel secure and safe, the more she became avoidant. Ironically, we both had some abandonment wounds, but we adopted very different strategies to stop from getting hurt again.

My second love

I was still very anxious when I fell for my second love. She was an avoidant as well. I was so infatuated with this girl that I never knew what time of day it was. She was stunningly beautiful, smart, successful, and funny. I couldn't believe my luck. To this day, I still haven't come across someone as avoidant as her. Both of us had similar abandonment issues and ended up choosing very different paths.

My third long-term girlfriend

Notice how I didn't say my third love? That's because I never loved her. I hadn't recovered from breaking up with my second love, so I ended up in a relationship to take the pain away. Rather than taking responsibility and working on myself, I got with someone more anxious than me. Finally, someone more fucked up than I was. She was so anxious she made me avoidant. I went from one extreme to another. I went from dating extremely avoidant women to extremely anxious women. Things went to shit, and she cheated on me. I guess I had that fucking coming.

The next love

The best relationship I have had to date and the relationship/breakup that inspired my channel and this book. She was somewhat secure but leaning-avoidant. I was somewhat secure but still leaning-anxious. I had done some work on myself. I could communicate better, but my anxiety got on top of me sometimes. When I felt incredibly anxious—guess what happened! She became extremely avoidant. What's that saying? The definition of madness is doing the same shit over and over and expecting a different result. If you look that up on Google, it may have me listed as an example of what not to fucking do.

Fast forward to today. I consider myself secure, leaning slightly anxious. I can far more effectively screen out bad attachment styles that do not match what I seek in a partner. That means far fewer candidates are available, but the remaining ones are much more compatible with me.

So why discuss attachment styles? Because it's all about you! The key theme throughout this book to help you break up with your breakup is taking ultimate responsibility for everything that happens to you and responding healthily to how you feel. Your first response might be to blame your ex for everything that happened. Remember, if you had their traumas, you would act the same way. The best way to avoid people who act like your ex, is to do the work on yourself and move on. By doing so, you will naturally attract more suitable romantic partners. This may be the most brutal chapter in the book, so hold on to your back teeth.

Case study: Extreme Attachment Styles – The Story of Malon and Dan

Malon, a former client of mine, was the most anxious dumpee I worked with. She was 35 and in a long-distance relationship. By her description, he was highly avoidant. In fact, his avoidance seemed to be directly proportional to Malon's anxiousness.

Anxious and avoidant attachment styles attract like a dog to their own vomit. I know! I just read that back to myself and even I threw up in my mouth a little bit.

Disgusting metaphors aside, anxious and avoidants find each other irresistible. Both are incredibly insecure. The anxious person constantly worries the relationship will end; thus, they are exceptionally needy. This neediness is relationship cancer. It's not the partner's responsibility to soothe this. The more needy someone is, especially with an avoidant, the more they are pushed away. Thus, they eventually end the relationship. For the anxious, the very thing they did to prevent the relationship from ending is causing the breakup.

Malon always felt out of control in the relationship. She would try to gain control by travelling to her partner more than he did to her. She would take him to couples therapy. She was prepared to give everything for him, whereas he scarcely gave anything back—hardly a fair exchange. Sadly, with an avoidant (her partner), the more you try to fix things, the more they recoil.

Avoidants do want intimacy, but it terrifies them. Closeness feels suffocating to the point they want to be as far away as possible. They value extended periods of alone time to process their feelings. This, to an anxious, feels like they are emotionally unavailable.

Dan, Malon's ex-boyfriend, couldn't be any less compatible with her (based on her description of him). The more she wanted, the more he resisted. After being with Malon for two years, the thought of the relationship developing or becoming more intimate threatened him. For him, a long-distance relationship was perfect. He had plenty of space to process his feelings. For Malon, she had to be closer or else she was anxious about losing him.

Both attachment styles are as fucked up as each other (in their own unique way). Malon believes she is too much for her partners. Therefore, she seeks partners who will reinforce this belief. An avoidant is a perfect partner to confirm her confirmation bias; the more intense she was, the more avoidant Dan became. Dan believed he needed to be more for his partners in relationships. This is the narrative he has told himself. Therefore, he sought partners who reinforced this belief.

An anxious is the perfect partner to confirm his confirmation bias.

This toxic dynamic allows both to reinforce their unhealthy attachment styles. The anxious will continue to believe they are too much, and the avoidant will continue to believe they are not enough. This is why they attract each other so well. Both are looking to validate their self-doubts.

Malon's attachment style perceived this threat to the relationship, so she turned everything up to eleven to salvage it. Ironically, her intense efforts and need to re-establish control expedited the breakup. The more control she tried to get, the less she had. Malon and Dan's relationship reinforced each other's core beliefs about themselves, and that is why it felt so fucking amazing in the beginning. They were mistaking their highs for happiness. When the honeymoon period ended, what was left? There was no foundation because their idea of love was built on their trauma.

Their opposite attachment styles spoke very different languages. It was like a German trying to teach English to a Japanese person. In other words, neither of them had the slightest fucking clue what the other was saying.

CONTROL YOUR REACTION

We can't control what happens to us, but we can control how we react.

You're not always in control of your feelings, but you are in control of your intentions and actions. I am all for exploring the science behind our limbic brain and how it makes us experience pain. However, I am also about as subtle as a grenade and will say, you can choose to not shit all over the floor when you're upset.

Our logical brain can give us tools that our limbic brain can't. Our limbic brain is wonderfully simple. Your limbic brain is like:

"I'm cold so let's find heat."

"I'm hungry so let's find food."

"I'm sad and alone, so I need my ex back or a rebound."

Our brain is very sophisticated. It's kept us alive since our distant ancestors wandered the earth millions of years ago. It's also as dumb and simple as a five-year-old who wants ice cream for dinner.

You're not a five-year-old, so stop acting like one. This is where self-care, accountability, and responsibility come in. You are everything you need. Why? Everyone in a relationship with you has one thing in common. You! You are the common denominator in everything you do, and the radical acceptance of that fact will help you break up with your breakup.

Choosing to act in a way that will benefit you despite every nerve in your body screaming at you to contact your ex is where the real magic lies.

I am not saying this is easy, but brute force will not help you. You will be motivated to find food, shelter, and love. These are carnal and powerful incentives. I've certainly slipped up a few times when dieting and I'm desperate for a doughnut. The next thing I know I've eaten 12 Krispy Kremes. That was fun! I felt like shit afterwards—the sugar rush was not good for my body. But I learned a good lesson that I had to have some self-control during moments like this. If I don't, then I will suffer in the future.

And yes, it's fucking hard to defer gratification or to not give in to our addictions. Love is an addiction, and the breakup is the withdrawal that comes with savage symptoms. But maybe we can make our childlike limbic brain and breakup symptoms a little easier by changing the metrics we measure ourselves with.

Accepting this part of the process sucks, but with goals in mind, will override your limbic brain. It will tell you you're lonely and make you desperate to reach out to your ex, but you must self-parent here.

> "When we choose the wrong measurement, we get the wrong behaviour."
>
> — James Clear, *Atomic Habits*

WHAT DOES IT MEAN TO SELF-PARENT?

Self-parenting fills in the gaps of care one did not receive during childhood, often resulting in feelings of unworthiness, shame, self-hatred, etc. These feelings are the result of emotionally absent, neglectful, or abusive caregivers. While you can never have a re-do your of your childhood, you can, as an adult, heal your inner child.

Why self-parent?

After lacking supportive relationships with adults as a child, people grow up to have low self-esteem, self-doubt, self-sabotage, etc. A healing experience with your parent may only happen if your parent is ready and able to participate. Even if they try to heal things now, there may be grief from your childhood. Self-parenting is a way to honour your childhood by building a healthy relationship within yourself to feel safe, heard, and loved.

If you choose to measure your worth based on your relationship status, then I do not doubt there's a five-year-old dickhead in your limbic brain. When that impulsive prick screams for a connection with your ex, you're likely to give in. If you realign your values to helping others or indulging in a hobby, you will begin to focus on yourself as your own entity with wants and desires. You can begin to make self-parenting decisions a little easier.

Instead of eating a box of 12 doughnuts, do 12 push-ups and eat some fruit. Keeping the metrics you gave yourself after you were dumped will keep you stuck in the breakup mud for a very long time. These new metrics give you just enough breathing room to step back and examine your situation and ultimately heal. Get *you* back.

Solitude and the self

Miyamoto Musashi (1584) was a Japanese rōnin, philosopher, and strategist born during a period of civil war. He is renowned for his storytelling abilities and unique swordsmanship and undefeated record of 61 duels. He emphasised that techniques are less important than the overall goal. The same fighting principles apply to not only conflict but also existence. Musashi put his observations into *The Dokkōdō* (The Path of Aloneness), expressing an ascetic and honest view of life. The most important message for you from these writings is:

"Do not seek pleasure for its own sake."

And what have you been doing for the sake of pleasure? Fawning over your ex.

His relentless pursuit of mastery over the self, made Musashi a badass. One key component was solitude and practising stillness in a world of violence and unrest. He walked a path of solitude, not in a conventional sense, but in his mind.

Musashi's philosophy emphasised solitude as a path to self-discovery and self-improvement. For him, solitude sharpened his mind and body without distraction, honing his skills and understanding himself away from distraction, noise and judgment. He also found clarity in understanding his strengths and weaknesses.

"Think lightly of yourself and deeply of the world."

– Miyamoto Musashi

What Musashi was getting at was observing and understanding the world while remaining humble. As I've mentioned, you must always maintain a sense of self. Whether in a relationship, fresh into a breakup, or single, your sense of self is an anchor in the turbulent sea of life. Your sense of self reminds you that your ex's actions are not about you. Your sense of self allows you to accept your ex for who they are and how they feel.

Sit still, breathe, and explore your sense of self in the solitude of your own mind. That's the battleground of where your healing will take place. This is the part that is about you. You've been dealt a shitty hand, and that sucks big, fat donkey balls. However, it's how you play the hand. If you play the hand well, you might have a better handle on your breakup.

Musashi wasn't some otherworldly deity who couldn't be killed. He accepted the world's rules, no matter how unfair or unjust, and found a way to harness the rules to his own advantage.

This is no different to a breakup. The rules fucking suck, and life is unfair at the best of times. Life is easier to navigate if you can find a way to operate within the rules.

People mistake their dopamine highs for happiness. However, these highs are fleeting. The more highs we have, the more we chase them. The more we chase them, the more unfulfilling they are. What is really happening? We're avoiding pain. We're avoiding our inner demons. We're avoiding looking for happiness inwards.

But hey, why would you do that?

You've never had to. Most of us have family, friends, hobbies, and addictions to soothe our pain. I'm not saying friends, family, or hobbies are bad (addictions can be), but when was the last time you switched everything off and sat still?

Challenge

Close this book and close your eyes. How long can you sit still before you itch to read on or open your phone? Start slowly and allow yourself just five minutes with no other distractions.

What thoughts are coming into your mind?

Thoughts coming during any period of self-reflection are normal. Try not to suppress them. Be curious about the thought and what the thought is trying to tell you. Write these thoughts down.

If you found yourself reaching for your phone, this may be a sign of you running from your thoughts and emotions. It may also be a sign of needing a dopamine hit from the pocket sized delivery system.

Sitting still and allowing your thoughts and feelings to do their thing is a great step to help you recover. They're not there to hurt you, they are there to alert you to the fact something is wrong. Embrace them.

Emotional pain is far more acute than happiness because emotional pain is there to keep us safe. Humans aren't built for happiness; we're built for survival. The happiness we're told we can have goes against our natural biology and is unsustainable.

Anecdotally speaking, why is it that the more we're told to be happy, the more unhappy we become? Is it because if we feel down and we're not happy according to modern day standards, we're somehow a failure?

Have you ever seen someone close to you doing well and you've felt inadequate and depressed, despite your life being just fine? No other animal does this or prioritises happiness. They prioritise survival and reproduction. These animals do not have time to think about happiness. They must secure their immediate physical survival. That is less of a problem for modern people and we therefore have too much time to create our own problems and call it unhappiness.

"Our brains can manage both positive and negative emotions simultaneously, relatively independent of one another. This provides a jump over those mental hurdles as you recognise 'the knowledge that dissatisfaction is not a personal failure'. Feeling down is not a shortcoming in need of immediate repair, but simply part of the fluctuations of life. It is, he concludes, 'what makes you human'."

– Rafael Euba

Allow me to translate.

Do not make decisions based on temporary emotions. Do not act impulsively because you're hurting. I refer you back to Nick's Law:

The breakup isn't about you, but it is your responsibility.

You don't have to act on your compulsions because you can take responsibility by breaking up with your breakup.

In *The Dokkōdō*, Musashi says, "Do not hold on to possessions that you no longer need." And I will go one better by stating you can't hold on to people either. Some people naturally drift apart, and that's okay. You can't negotiate with someone no longer emotionally and physically available. By holding on to them, you're letting go of yourself.

So talk yourself down from breaking no-contact. This is where your true power lies. This is where the seeds of growth take root. This is the way.

Musashi also said: 道においては死をいとわず思う

Which roughly translates to: "On the path, think not ill of death."

You might be thinking that means that it is okay to walk across the road without looking. What it really means is to live a full life knowing you will die. So, make the fucking most of the time you have. Don't waste it being hooked up on someone who does not want to be with you. I think one of the most painful parts to a breakup is the realisation that 'forever' isn't real.

ETERNAL LOVE IS NARCISSISTIC

Eternity is actually a narcissistic concept when you really think about it. I am referring to narcissistic thinking, and not narcissists per se. We can all adopt narcissistic thinking when in relationships or going through a breakup. When it comes to eternity or our love will last forever, there is an active assumption that your relationship or breakup, is somehow more special than anyone else's and beyond time itself. These narcissistic thoughts put you in a mindset of not having to make an effort to grow, change and take responsibility in the same way everyone else does.

Fantasy of eternal love, and the very denial of death, is an ultimate threat to narcissistic grandiosity. While the fantasy of eternal love and the denial of death may be a dreamy imagining of a lovestruck fool, in the narcissistic mindset it becomes grossly exaggerated and interferes with the reality of time and change.

Yet, we continue to believe our romantic relationships are special; our partners will never leave and we'll never be alone. Despite the evidence nothing is certain in life, we convince ourselves that love defies the odds.

Love conquers all, right?

Love is *never* enough. The only certainty in life is uncertainty. For your romantic relationships to be successful, you must be okay with this. Here's the kicker: without uncertainty, without the possibility of abandonment, love is conditional. If there aren't conditions to love then it loses its meaning! The very fact that it could end, that they could stop loving you, that nothing is certain, is what makes it feel so fucking good and meaningful.

Romantic love is hugely conditional, and those conditions can change at any time. The person who loves you one month can leave you the next. They go from your special someone to a complete fucking stranger. It's savage! The thing is it doesn't actually happen overnight. A breakup starts before it actually happens. It's death by a thousand cuts.

Repeat after me:

Amor Fati

Love your fate.

No matter what happens to you, own it, embrace it, and improve. Be okay with whatever happens and you will be free.

Momento Mori

You can die at any moment.

Armed with this, are you going to sit here wasting another second on someone no longer investing in you? Or will you think that one day you will no longer exist? If you're 35 years old, you're already technically middle aged. So, how much more time do you want to waste on someone who left you?

Our limited time in this world, and the uncertainty of life, gives us meaning. Thinking everything is certain and will last forever is entitled and meaningless! You're entitled to nothing! You're only entitled to the work you do on yourself, not the outcome you think you deserve. The second you drop the entitlement, the happier you will be.

Thought experiments:

1. Is our interconnectedness with others through artificial means like social media, leading us to being evermore disconnected with ourselves?

2. If we were better connected with ourselves, would we have better romantic relationships?

3. If we stopped trying to save the damsel and let them fucking save themselves, would books like this even need to exist?

Take home points:

It's okay to have baggage but don't allow the baggage to have you. The attachment style you formed as a child is a normal response to the relationship with your primary caregiver. You are not too much; you are enough. However, it is your responsibility to heal. Attachment styles are very much a thing so it's on you to not blame your childhood on the places you fail at in adulthood.

Your limbic lizard brain is largely in control of your emotions and cravings. It needs safety. However, it behaves like a spoiled child constantly shitting all over the floor when it wants something. Self-parenting and taking radical responsibility for everything that happens can go a long way to keeping that little prick in line.

If you keep measuring yourself by your relationship status, or the fact your ex dumped you, you will continue to fail. Measure yourself by the lessons you've learnt. Measure yourself by how you help others. Measure yourself by choosing to go to therapy. Measure yourself by understanding yourself.

Breakups are a path of solitude. This does not mean being totally alone, but rather, finding solitude in your own mind. This will help you find a sense of self. If you can find a sense of self, then you can find a new identity. As our identity is linked to our emotional survival, you will begin to recover far easier. Your new identity will replace the identity you so passionately attached to your ex.

Malon and Dan never took the time to heal. They found in each other a toxic reinforcement of their respective traumas. They never took the responsibility for their healing, so they outsourced it. Just like you and me, they are the common denominator in everything they do. The buck stops with them. If they fail to heal their own insecure attachment styles, it will follow them into future relationships. The lesson here is that you must participate in your own rescue.

Chapter 6

The Breakup Wasn't Up to You but It Is Your Responsibility

Taking responsibility was one of my most difficult but liberating experiences. Taking responsibility for emotions caused by rejection went against every fibre of my being. I wanted to be angry, and I wanted to blame my ex for leaving me and making me feel like shit. The harsh reality is my ex could only ever see things from her perspective. This is always okay.

For the longest time, I played the victim, saying shit like: "How can she throw our relationship away so easily?" and its ugly cousin "How could she do this to me?"

She wasn't doing anything to me—she wasn't trying to hurt me—she was merely doing what she felt was best for her. Sadly, I carried this narcissistic thought process around with me for almost a year, and it got me nowhere.

Here's the thing: you can invite someone to love you and then to join your journey. Hell, you can ask them to stay and work things out. But you can't make them do anything. Coercing, begging, or manipulating someone into staying in your life is transactional. Love at such a price is as hollow as your ex asking you to be friends after they dumped you. It would be like saying: "I love you" to someone just because they said it to you. This is a disorder of responsibility. Your ex is saying: "I no longer want this," and you're trying to frantically out-logic their feelings because you don't want to experience the emotions of a breakup.

Wanting to avoid the pain of a breakup is natural and completely normal. Our attachments run deep; we will go down swinging to protect them because we're designed to do that. We're also designed to find other attachments if the current one no longer works. Therefore, your ex is perfectly justified to feel how they feel. Ultimately, you are simply trying to save yourselves, but your strategy no longer aligns. This is precisely what happened with me and my ex. I saw logic in staying together, but she saw logic in walking away.

Realising I had no power over the situation, I had to choose how to respond. I could either: shit the bed, blame her for everything, blow up her phone, or stalk her social media (full transparency, the five-year-old driving my limbic brain like a fucking go-kart wanted to do this). I wanted to blame her for all my pain and anxiety.

But I couldn't do this.

I had to practice radical acceptance and take full responsibility for how I responded to my pain. It was time to put the five-year-old in my limbic brain down for a nap.

BAD SHIT HAPPENS

You're probably thinking this chapter just went on a massive side tangent, and whilst there are many stupid side tangents in this book because I was distracted by something shiny, I can assure you this isn't one of them, and it will make sense.

> "Imagine something worse than anything you've ever seen in a movie, read about, or heard about. Imagine something original. Pause in your reading and conjure this awful thing.
>
> Now, by virtue of the fact that you could conceive it, rest assured it has likely been done to someone because everything that a human being can do to another human being has been done. Acts of extraordinary horror and violence happen, and we cannot learn why they happen by looking at rare behaviour as if it is something outside ourselves. That idea you just conjured was in you, and thus it is part of us."
>
> – Gavin De Becker, *The Gift of Fear*

What De Becker is alluding to is… If you can conceive something then you can do it. If you can conceive dumping someone then you can do so. Say you are your ex for a moment, you would've dumped you too. I have a feeling you may be itching to delete this book or burn it but you're just proving my point and…

Haha, you already bought the book.

Everyone is capable of anything. From cheating, to rebounding, to monkey-branching, to murder (this is a bit excessive I don't recommend or condone this action). You may have said to yourself many times: "If anyone hurts (insert someone important to you here) I will be going to prison for murder." Between you and me, when someone threatened to hurt my dog once, I was ready to end the person in question. Thankfully, I was distracted and we all lived happily ever after.

Given the right conditions, anyone is capable of anything. Just as your ex is capable of loving you beyond all measure, they were also capable of dumping you when the relationship stopped working for them. You are equally capable of loving beyond all measure and dumping someone when it stops working for you.

The only difference in your situation is, you're the dumpee. This isn't your limbic brain's preferred outcome. Your preferred outcome is to stay with your partner. However, if the situation was reversed, you are more than capable of doing the same thing. Your partner committing the painful act from among many options (sticking it out, going to therapy) is a conceivable idea. It's happened to you. It's happened to your friends. A breakup is a pretty familiar occurrence, but it doesn't exist because it's meant to teach you about them. They are opportunities to teach you about *you*.

Your ex merely acts in a way which doesn't align with your morals and ethics. They act in a way aligned with their traumas and perceptions of reality. You, me, and your cat are not required to understand your ex's rationale, so you might as well give them the breakup. What other choice is there?

We all start from zero, and thus, we're just a product of nature and nurture. We're all guilty of being human, even the most evil and tyrannical of us. Please keep that in mind as I tell you the following.

Now, this is an extreme example of what not taking responsibility for the bad shit that happens to you can lead to. It's an example of blaming everyone and the world for your pain, and not taking responsibility. The following story isn't a reflection of my personal opinions or beliefs. Rather, it is an examination of what not taking responsibility can look like, and that someone else's actions are about their traumas, and not about the person on the receiving end of it. Much like when your ex dumped you. It was about them and their feelings. The narrative outlined in the story does not excuse anything, but it explains everything.

You never asked for the physical or mental trauma, but it will always be your responsibility to go through the process of feeling the pain, accepting it, levelling up and eventually moving on. How you respond to how you feel will always be the determining factor to your happiness or bitterness.

There was a young boy who loved his mother more than any other person in the world. Born to parents who were second cousins, he was at the mercy of physical genetic deformities. His parents, and grandparents were inbred in their small town. Three siblings preceded the young boy, but they all sadly died as infants, likely due to the inbreeding. The boy's mother doted on him, and they went on to form the closest bond a mother and son could have, short of experiencing sexual abuse.

As the boy grew, he was prone to outbursts of violence and would demand subservience from his fellow students. His teachers labelled him wilful, lazy, and arrogant. Obsessive, self-centred and incapable of having his opinions challenged by anyone, the red flags were apparent from infancy.

135

His father, an alcoholic and wife-beater, would frequently attack the boy with tyrannical violence. The boy learned to be silent and suppress his tears as his father mercilessly lashed him with a whip.

The conditions were perfect to create a monstrous serial killer. An overly doting mother with whom he had an over-bonded relationship and a distant but dominating father (acting out his own traumas) brutalising him with violence.

When the boy was 14, his father died of a heart attack. The tyrannical toxic alpha father figure had released the boy and his mother from their torment. At last, the boy and his mother could begin to heal and live in some peace.

Four years later, the boy's mother sadly died from breast cancer. The boy who had always worshipped his mother was destroyed and could not cope with her death.

The boy, now a young man, suffered rejection after rejection. He couldn't get into the schools he wanted, and he couldn't get the girls he wanted. His mental health would rapidly deteriorate, and he would spew hate on anyone who didn't agree with or understand him. He very much adopted a victim's mindset and blamed everyone and the world for how he felt, and for the state of his life. His physical ailments he inherited from his parents, and the generations of inbreeding only got worse as he got older. He was skinny, frail, shallow chested and quite often unable to defend himself physically.

Even the army, who were desperate to recruit new soldiers and therefore would take on almost anyone, rejected him because they deemed him too frail for combat.

Most armies were quite forgiving. If you could stand and fire a weapon, then you were typically more than suitable to be part of the operation of a human shield.

The young man, as frail as he was, could certainly walk and fire a weapon, but the army doctor saw his deformities and rejected his application.

Undeterred, the young man signed up to another army that had even more forgiving requirements and he was sent off to war. Surprisingly, the young man was a competent soldier, but his fellow soldiers found him to be a lone wolf and a little odd. He would once again spew hate against anyone or a group of people that did not align with his worldview.

As with most people in the young man's position, he found himself to be the laughing stock of his platoon, and he may have been the victim of sexual abuse due to his genetic deformities, in his genital area. A psychologist at the time said the man in question would attempt to display brute strength, hate, and rage at any opportunity in an attempt to overcompensate for his deformed manhood and his frailty.

Add to that his savage childhood and we've got the genesis of a mass murderer, gathering strength like a storm on the horizon before it unleashes its fury upon the world.

This abused, rejected, formless, faceless boy would go on to be a powerful public speaker, the leader of what became the biggest political party in his country, and he would set into motion the most significant event in modern history, which changed the world forever. That little boy was Adolf Hitler, and we all fucking know how that turned out!

My point is we're all fucked up. We're all influenced by our trauma and beliefs. If you had the same trauma and experiences as Hitler, there is a fair chance you would've acted the exact same way.

Their traumas influence everyone you know. We're all simply fucked up in our own unique way. The next time you ask yourself, "Why did they hurt me so badly?" remind yourself it was never about hurting you. They acted upon their own bullshit.

Do you think Adolf Hitler thought of himself as evil or that he was doing anything wrong? Go watch the documentary *Hitler's Secret Sex Life* and World War II makes a lot of fucking sense from his demented perception of reality. He thought the rest of the world was fucked, and he was the hero.

We're all the fucking heroes in our own story. Your ex is very much the hero in their story when they dumped you. From their perspective, dumping you made all the sense in the world. You can't change this.

The only thing separating us from the angels and insects is how we choose to respond to our feelings and take responsibility for what happens to us. Perhaps the most famous psychological study of Hitler was done by Henry A. Murray, former director of the Harvard Psychological Clinic.[11] Dr. Murray points out that though there is very little information available about Hitler's youth he is said to have been sickly and frail. His father was "tyrannical" and physically abusive.

Here we can begin to see how Hitler, as a young boy, was overpowered by his father and confronted with a situation he could not control, except by controlling his own emotions and actions. Murray suggests Hitler's hatred for his father fuelled his hatred of Jews, who, after his father died when Adolf was only fourteen, served as scapegoats for his residual fury. According to Murray, Hitler was "counteractive" and primarily motivated by revenge and resentment in response to emotional wounding and feelings of inferiority.

Narcissism is a compensatory defence against these painful wounds and feelings. Adolf Hitler projected his extreme traumas because he was not able to take responsibility for how he felt. I think we can all agree that he chose wrongly and is the very definition of evil.

Your ex likely projected their bullshit onto you and now you're projecting yours onto them. Your preferred outcome is probably some reconciliation but I doubt they feel the same. Regardless of your situation. Don't do what Hitler did and defer responsibility for how you feel. His disorder of responsibility sealed his fate.

> "You have power over your own mind—not outside events. Realise this and you will find strength."
>
> — Marcus Aurelius

If you take anything from this book, let it be that you very much have the ability to choose how you respond to your feelings. It's not just a choice, it's a personal responsibility. Trying to wipe out any country, or group of people who do not align with your narcissistic thought process isn't the way, trust me. The paperwork alone is a fucking nightmare! Respect people act the way they do because that is who they are. Your ex is no different and you have zero control over their actions.

The truly scary thing is, anyone is capable of being the next Hitler if the conditions are right. If we are threatened, deprived, or endangered we are as capable as the most blood-thirsty lion. Rather than judging your ex for whatever horrible shit they did, step back and remember they are acting on their traumas.

They're guilty of being human.

> "How much more damage anger and grief do than the things that cause them."
>
> — Marcus Aurelius

They said it couldn't be done people, but you just got two Marcus Aurelius quotes in the space of two paragraphs. I'm smashing writing this chapter!

Hitler began life the same way as you and I. Your ex began life the same way as you and I. What happens after birth is a roll of the dice. Our experiences shape our personalities.

There is nothing you can do to change how your ex was raised. Their circumstances and experiences made them who they are. If you acquire a victim mentality under this guise then you stop taking ownership of your perspective.

BEWARE THE VICTIM MENTALITY

A victim mentality is a personality trait where people view themselves as victims. They often feel like they lack control over the events in their life. To stop playing the victim, you have to take ownership of your worldview. The power is in your hands (or should we say, your mind)!

Causes:

People may develop a victim mentality due to negative experiences. These include:

- Betrayal
- Emotional pain
- Trauma
- Manipulative tendencies

Although it's not always in your control as to what happens to you, it's possible to practice resilience. By being resilient, you gain the ability to recover from misfortune or painful experiences. This means being mentally tough.

So, grab it by the fucking balls!

Let's look at some ways you can sharpen your resilience and reshape your outlook to be positive and proactive.

Be aware of limiting beliefs:

Your experiences and memories make up your perceptions and beliefs. You interpret and define everything based on your outlook and internal monologues. You can be led to self-sabotage if your thoughts are negative or disempowering. These negative thought patterns also cause feelings of helplessness.

The first step in being able to reshape these thoughts is to know they exist.

Most people never silence their inner chatter, but it does pay to take moments of self-reflection or meditation to acknowledge your thoughts. When you do so, you are likely to become aware of whether or not you have negative self-talk or a positive and uplifting inner voice.

Once you are aware of your thoughts, you can take the time to reflect on where they come from. Think about your past and what made you think this way. Then, focus on stopping negative thoughts in your mind. Remember that you can silence limiting beliefs and transform them into confidence. It comes down to shifting your narrative (the stories you tell yourself).

Deal with anger:

Anger may often feel like one's second nature, forcing you to feel there is nothing you can do to control it. That's why it's vital to acknowledge and redirect anger— if it remains unchecked, anger can evolve into resentment, stress, and irrational behaviours.

If you try to rationalise anger, then it can leave you feeling like a victim. This often happens because people think of how things "should be" or focus on desiring a feeling of "fairness".

Instead, reshape the narrative and remind yourself that people typically act in their own self-interest. In many situations, whatever has happened to you may be collateral damage and is not personal.

By reshaping how you define situations, you can let go of anger. Rather, you can redirect that energy into productivity or understanding a lousy situation to ensure you are never again put in that position.

Celebrate wins:

Stop defining wins as big or small. Celebrate everything positive!

The more you take note of your wins and think positively about them, the more confidence you can breed. With more confidence comes less space for victimhood because you realise you are the only person in charge of your life.

A significant aspect of celebrating small or big wins comes down to self-compassion. Treat yourself the way you want others to treat you.

Walk away:

Don't be afraid to walk away if you are in a negative situation once or repeatedly. You get to control who you spend time with.

And, if you are in situations where you are surrounded by negative energy and can't just walk away (i.e., in a team meeting at work), then try your best to let go and not take things personally.

Practice gratitude:

A major foundation of the victim mentality is a sense of lacking something. When you feel something is missing, it's easy to get stuck in a trail of negative thoughts and self-pity.

Instead, when you focus on the blessings in your life and practice gratitude, you can find yourself in a positive mindset.

Thinking positively and focusing on the good often breeds more positivity. After all, it's all a state of mind.

If you can take responsibility, you will become bulletproof and have a far better outlook on life. Give your ex what they want and let them think happy happy thoughts forever. Show your ex you will be okay with or without them. Be stoic as fuck, agree to the breakup, and give the gift of silence. Regardless of whether they reach out or not, you will be on the path of recovery. Marcus Aurelius figured this shit out two millennia ago. They were cool and stoic. Be like them.

RESPONSIBILITY AND GROWTH EAT HOPE FOR BREAKFAST

"Fear can hold you prisoner. Hope can set you free."

– *The Shawshank Redemption*

Before I launch into this section of the book, I want to go on record and say that *The Shawshank Redemption* is one of the greatest movies ever made, and I fucking love it. However, what I quoted about fear and hope is utter bullshit. I have been telling people on my YouTube channel, my Facebook support group and my one-to-one clients the following for years:

"Hope is an approximation created by you. It does not exist. It is very much a manifestation of the belief that we can influence people or events outside of our control. The second you understand this and change your mindset, you will be far better off. If you can say to yourself: If scenario A happens, I'm cool with it. If scenario B happens, I'm also cool with it. You will be able to move forward. Stop hoping and focus on your growth. It's a much better investment of your time."

Here's the thing about hope. It will keep you stuck in the place making you sick. It will keep you in the relationship with your breakup because, in your limbic brain, the relationship is salvageable. Hope begins as soothing medicine soothing your anxiety at the beginning of the breakup. It is still very fresh. Maybe your ex is just angry and needs to calm down.

So, why can't you let go of someone who dumped you and hurt you? Why hold on to your ex for weeks or months even though you wish to move on?

Many dumpees want to know if there's still hope their ex will come back. They want to know if their ex will think about them, miss them, or want to reunite. What such dumpees avoid is information disproving these hopes. They look solely for ways to reconnect with their ex, and this is very, very dangerous because dumpees have no control over their ex's thoughts and feelings. They had a strong influence during the relationship but not after the breakup because their ex had painted a black picture of them and held on to the negative feelings he or she had created before the breakup.

Therefore, we can't let go of our ex because there is still hope deep inside. We hope our ex will come back and take our pain away and fulfil our cravings.

We hope because:

- It gives us strength and positivity
- It gives us control over unwanted situations
- It gives us the courage to keep going

Hope doesn't change the outcome.

Granted, I've just shat all over hope, but it's not a completely wasted tool. The hope that you will start to feel better might be just the ticket to getting yourself out of bed and putting your running shoes on. If that leads to your growth, then I'm all fucking for it. But I'm going to propose a radical shift in philosophy. Abandon hope and embrace growth. Staying the same is no longer an option because it's too fucking painful. That's what got you into this mess in the first place, and if you stay where you are, you will carry all this bullshit into the next chapter of your life. That will lead to another breakup, and I'll book you in for a breakup coaching session.

For breakups, hope is the worst thing we can experience. We don't know if our ex will come back. And because we don't know what will happen, we hope for it. This prolongs our healing time, makes us get addicted to our exes, and we become dependent on them.

Here are five reasons why hope after the breakup is dangerous:

1. It raises your expectations

2. It makes you feel good for a moment and bad the next

3. It becomes an addiction

4. It prolongs the time it takes to get over your ex

5. It stops you from reflecting on your flaws and hinders self-growth

So, why waste energy on someone who doesn't want you? Taking radical responsibility for how you respond gives you the power and the freedom to grow.

"With great responsibility comes great power."

– Mark Manson,
The Subtle Art of Not Giving a Fuck

For me to let go of the bullshit that contributed to my breakup, I had to own it. Yes, my ex had her issues, but so did I. I could either grow or regress. I could choose the victim mindset or the student mindset. Choosing the student mindset means acknowledging my emotional baggage and being vulnerable enough to share it. I was like:

"Hey, my name is Nick. I've had chronic anxiety my whole life, and it torpedoed more than one relationship. In fact, in every long-term and meaningful relationship I've had, I was the one who was dumped. The common denominator in all cases is me, so I guess I've got some work to do. I really want to blame my exes and tell you what bitches they all are, but I'm working on myself and that kind of responsibility doesn't afford me such a luxury."

Here's the thing about your reality and mine. It's all fucking subjective. In your head, you might be thinking your ex is an evil, narcissistic, complete fucking hobo with camel breath. You make yourself the hero of your story. To your ex, you're the one who didn't listen, didn't give them enough attention, and took the relationship for granted. Whether this is true or not doesn't fucking matter; the results are the same.

The objective reality is you're no longer together, and this hurts like a motherfucker. It's the worst fucking feeling in the world, and you just want to curl up in a ball on the floor and die.

The story you now tell yourself is that you cannot grow or evolve without a relationship with your partner because it's fucking with your identity. And your prick of a limbic brain is telling you that you can't do it because it wants you to go back to where it last felt safe, which was with your ex, and it's using hope to manipulate you into staying exactly where you are.

Getting unstuck and growing is a bitch. I often hear people in my Facebook breakup group saying they were doing great a year post-breakup. Then, one day, they wake up and feel like they're back to the moment of the breakup. They're all panic, dread, and anxiety. Then, they start stalking their ex on social media. This is called a 'Breakup Relapse' because it's your limbic brain's last attempt to get your ex back. I had about six relapses a year after my breakup.

In the context of a breakup, there is no bigger growth killer than a Breakup Relapse. All the hope you had in the beginning is back, but in Dolby Atmos surround sound. You've made great gains and progress in many areas of your life, but everything starts to slow down. You're not losing weight as quickly anymore, the novelty of new hobbies, friends and adventures is wearing off, and maybe you've had a few dates, but nothing pans out. Everything is just a little harder and slowing down. The effort is no longer worth the reward.

This is where your brain sees its opportunity to fuck you over, and it's like, "Hey, this no-contact and working on yourself thing was fun, but it's getting a little difficult. Let's contact the ex and see if they want to be friends now. And by friends, I mean lovers because that would be far easier than this get-you-back bullshit."

Sound familiar?

Don't listen to the five-year-old prick in your head. This halfway point is where so many get stuck. This is the tipping point between working on yourself and wanting your ex back or working on yourself and not wanting your ex back. This is where you must choose to take the short-term hope and fuck it off to suffer long-term but take the brutal growing pains of prosperity.

One of the most famous examples is Thomas Edison, who invented the carbon telephone transmitter, light bulb, and phonograph. In fact, it took 1,000 unsuccessful attempts before he created the first light bulb. Imagine if he stopped at 999. So close to a breakthrough yet so far. Edison chose the long-term growth pains rather than settling for a substandard filament that may have been less efficient and durable. Worse still, what if he had just abandoned the project? What if you did the same with your breakup recovery?

Growth fucking hurts, but it's far less painful than placing your hope on someone who does not want you.

As long as you blame your ex, parents, friends, dog, and the weather for how you feel, you will remain in an abyss of anxiety and low self-esteem. If you never take responsibility, you'll never run out of people to blame.

People often accuse me of being unsympathetic when I say it's your responsibility for your feelings. Nothing could be further from the truth. In fact, it took me a long time to realise the only way forward is *through*, which means owning your shit.

For me, rather than fantasising about my ex coming back, I realised that blaming my ex for how I felt, imprisoned me. I thought: "If my ex did come back, who would she find? The guy she dumped, or who took responsibility for how he felt and levelled up?" There was only one answer: leave her alone and don't worry about her actions.

I am not saying my anxiety disappeared overnight, but taking responsibility for how I felt, no matter the cause, gave me direction. A year of therapy, meditation, journaling, training my arse off in the gym, and cold showers was my way of taking responsibility. No matter how I felt, I would ensure I completed my daily routine. Whilst I was focused on my routine, I wasn't focused on my ex. Sure, thoughts of her occupied my head daily, but my response was my choice and responsibility. I was never going to contact her despite how much I wanted to. I would never reconcile with her because I knew she wouldn't change the things she got wrong.

There is peace and simplicity in accepting these types of situations.

I started to flourish once I knew we were no longer right for each other.

So, you may think my saying: "Take responsibility for your shit" is harsh but it's the opposite. I am saying the sooner you take responsibility, the sooner you will start to feel better. The sooner you start digging yourself out of the hole your ex left you in, the sooner you climb back to the top, hardened by the descent into hell and humbled by the climb to the top. I am not saying I escaped without pain or scars. On the contrary, I went through the emotional no man's land.

I entered made of putty and emerged calved in wood.

The crazy thing is everyone around me leapt to my defence. Although I tried to give an unbiased account of what happened and remain accountable for my part in the breakup, no one stepped forward to keep me honest. My parents took my side without question (but that is their job). My friends backed me up. My colleagues said I could do better. I needed clarification and their partisan support was not helping me.

Bless their hearts.

I could not ask for a better support system, but I found this to be counterproductive to my healing. I started to believe what they were telling me, which detracted from taking responsibility.

What I needed was unbiased advice, so I sought coaching and therapy. Man, there is no advice like unbiased advice. When someone has no skin in the game, they can break you down like a cheap car held together by rust. There were times I was crying my eyes out after a therapy session because my therapist uncovered issues I was fiercely denying. My therapist saw through me. Over months, they dismantled my bullshit until the truth was left.

After my, shall we say… awakening, it was like someone opened the window to a stagnant room and let fresh air in. Ultimately, the old version of me had to die to be reborn as a new version. The old version was sent back to the pit it spawned in.

Once I realised I'm responsible for how I feel, I started to move on.

The problem with responsibility is it's like kryptonite. It means looking within ourselves and being honest with the parts we hate the most. Your ex dumping you makes you self-doubt, self-deprecate, and question your self-worth. The natural course of action is to defer responsibility and deny, deny, deny there is anything wrong with you.

But I say: *fuck that*.

Confront the pain! It's only once you confront pain, you can heal. Confronting my pain came in the way of examining what I got wrong. For months, I pondered why my ex dumped me when we had a good relationship. Then I started to ask myself the brutal question "What am I shit at?" The reflection that looked back disgusted me. The things I were shit at provided additional kindling for the breakup—ego, anxiousness, the need to be right all the time, and so on.

Instead of listing the reasons why my ex was being so unreasonable, which diminished my responsibility and power over my life, I decided to accept responsibility for everything.

I accepted responsibility for how I responded to my ex's actions, how I felt and for how I healed moving forward. I stopped asking why my ex did what she did, instead I simply accepted who she was and that she did what she did. I had no power over anything she said, did or felt.

 I decided to go to therapy and it was brutal.

Signing up for therapy is purposely putting yourself into the most uncomfortable position you can imagine. You are paying someone to uncover everything you're shit at, and to do a deep dive on your childhood trauma.

Confronting *my* pain was an admission of: I am not as good as I think I am. It was letting go of the hero in my story and allowing my identity to be challenged.

A breakup is very much the pursuit of truth:

Why did my ex dump me?

- What did I do wrong?
- What did my ex do?
- Were we ever meant to be?

The pursuit of the truth requires absolute candour. This is fucking brutal. You will need to take full accountability of everything you got wrong. Poke and probe what you're sensitive to.

Taking responsibility is the ultimate act of self-love. It's only when we take responsibility we can gradually change and become better:

- Taking responsibility is wanting to change.
- Taking responsibility is getting out of your own way.
- Taking responsibility is accepting reality.
- Taking responsibility is admitting you can do better.
- Taking responsibility is mastering you and your bullshit.

Taking responsibility is the hardest thing you will likely do because it's admitting you're not as good as you thought. It will likely highlight your anxiety. Taking responsibility for your actions is never easy, especially as they have consequences. But honestly, people who blame others for their failures never overcome them, nor do they run out of other people to blame. They move from problem to problem.

To reach your potential, you must continually improve. You can only do that if you take responsibility for your actions and learn from your mistakes. You could start taking responsibility by making one small change in your life. If you make enough small changes, you will see sooner or later that the big changes you wanted seemingly happened overnight.

A small change I made was to set aside twenty minutes every day to read. I went from reading nothing to a few pages every day. Over the course of six months, I had finished eight books which had a profound effect on me. My mindset started to shift from a victim to a student's mindset. This led to other changes such as only focusing on the things I could control. The happy side effect was a decrease in anxiety and increase in discovering new adventures and friends.

THE BREAKUP WASN'T UP TO YOU

This section of the book is going to be rough. I want you to put yourself in your ex's shoes. You may feel angry or betrayed but now it's time to heal. I've said it before but their breaking up with you wasn't up to you. I have written the next part from the dumper's perspective to show you.

Now, let's enter the dumper's mind:

> "God, he's so fucking quiet. Why is he always so quiet? Look at him—he can barely look at *me* anymore. He can barely look at himself either. What happened to the kind and gentle man he was before? Oh, how he held and stroked my hair. Now, it's like we're two strangers forced to share a bed every night. I tried to tell him how work was but he just shrugged. Shrugged! I feel like a piece of furniture he walks past and sometimes catches his leg on and suddenly remembers I'm here. I no longer feel safe. I no longer feel heard. We used to be so great. There was a time I would've walked through barbed wire to be with them, but recently, I've not felt it. He was so attentive initially, always listening to understand and holding space for me. He was so passionate about his career and hobbies, but all he does now is come home from work and complain. I'm dying inside! He won't

let me in; he shuts me down whenever I communicate my feelings. He makes me feel like the loneliest person in the world, even though he is next to me.

Today, I tried to tell him that our relationship is slipping. I tried to tell him how I miss dating him and our banter. He looked at me and told me it's just in my head and everything is okay. He didn't acknowledge my sadness or my concerns. I suggested couples therapy and he laughed. I suggested regular date nights. He said he was too tired. I suggested we make time for sex and intimacy. He again said he is too tired.

It's been six months. I can't do this anymore and I've changed. Once I've changed, I'm a different person and I can't love him the way I used to. I still care about him, and I don't want to hurt him but is this man going to be my husband? Is he going to be the father of my children? Is he going to be my biggest fan, or just a cold pair of shoulders in bed?

I've realised we were not compatible from day one and that's partly my fault. I should've screened better and realised we wasn't right for each other. We bonded over trauma, nothing more. He told me he never wanted to get married, but I do. He bottles up his feelings and I want to have open communication and vulnerability. Maybe, in the beginning, it was just an act from him, and the mask finally slipped.

Now I can see the real him. He's not a bad guy and I still care for him. He's just not for me anymore. I must put myself first now because there is no future with this man. He has shown me what I don't want in a relationship. I don't want to hurt him, but this is the best choice for the both of us. The relationship doesn't work, and it never did. I don't feel the way I should for the relationship we share together. My heart broke the night he told me everything was in my head but that wasn't his fault. I chose this man. I chose a reflection of me and that is what I need to change. It is up to me to. I love him but I don't love the relationship we share and that is what I am leaving."

If you're reading this from the perspective of the dumpee (as I suspect), you may have created some conditions which facilitated the dumper's choice. You will never possess the ability, and nor should you, to make up someone's mind. They didn't leave you! They left the relationship. You had zero control—which is terrifying—but here's the kicker: you never had control in the first place.

A relationship can end at any time, for any reason, by either partner.

Step back and ask yourself: If I were my ex with their trauma, experiences, worldview, and feelings, would I make the same choice? If you answer "No" to that question, quite frankly, you're lying and won't get what this book is trying to teach. I'm not saying your ex never played a part in your breakup, but this book isn't about your ex or trying to understand them. This book is to get you to break up with your breakup. This requires radical acceptance of the truth.

So, what can you control? Your recovery.

SELF-AUDIT

This is where I must be brutally honest with myself. My last relationship was doomed from the start. My ex and I almost started a relationship six years previously. It wasn't the right time; I had no confidence and she rejected me. I wanted her so badly that, when she got back in contact with me, she validated my whole existence, and I didn't even question it. Still licking my wounds from being cheated on three years earlier, and the woman I always wanted reaching out after six years, I jumped in headfirst and to hell with the shallow waters, with the rocky seabed lurking underneath. There was no screening, no acknowledgment of red flags and no real thought of what it means to take on a woman with a three-month-old baby.

The first time we almost got together was in 2010 (I can't remember exactly when because my brain starts losing its functionality after hours of writing and I am well past this as I write this sentence). I get distracted by something shiny, chase it down the street for three hours and then complain I am not progressing. Anyway, back then I had no confidence. I convinced myself that I was so ugly and unattractive that I could never get a woman. I was too stupid to realise my ex wanted to spend time with me.

I couldn't unfuck myself because of my chronic anxiety and I made her out to be this unattainable thing in my head. I convinced myself that beautiful women were only attracted to gigachad men––tall, dark, handsome Superman abs, Popeye arms, and so on. I'm just shy of being six feet tall. I kept myself in good shape and had decent arms on me. So even when I conformed to my own terrible metrics, I still fucked myself because I valued her opinions of me more than I valued my own.

Fast forward to 2016 and she was still unattainable. I never loved myself enough to realise that I could get women or a woman like her. I employed her to love me because I couldn't love myself.

That, my friends, is a responsibility most of us must bear. It was but the tip of the iceberg of shit that I never took ownership of. A shitberg of shitty values if you will.

We had a very good relationship. I was lacking in some key areas, but so was she (I will get into my deficiencies in a bit). Let's do some ex-bashing, shall we? All jokes aside, this book isn't about sticking it to my ex, and I will never say bad things about her. However, it is essential to point out that it takes two people to get together and two to break up. I chose her and she chose me. My deficiencies reflected her, and her deficiencies reflected me. If she got with an anxious man that had no fucking clue how to love himself, what does that say about her? It would suggest she also didn't know how to love herself in the way that she needed to. I was propping her up as much as she was propping me up. It seemed we both suffered from the same disease. We both had a disorder of responsibility and outsourced that responsibility to each other. Both were too concerned about being right, operating from our own worldviews and traumas; it became Me vs Her rather than Us versus the Problem.

And here's the real problem: you already know everything about yourself and your situation. Everything I have said, from ripping off other authors, philosophers, and quotes from people I've forgotten the names of to telling random stories that make my point, you always know you are your own worst problem. You see the red flags. You either ignore them or try to love them. You measure your shitty opinion of yourself against others. You take a low-ball offer because you do not love yourself enough.

The shitty thing that will piss you off is the fact you choose your partner because they reflect who you are.

I wasn't boyfriend of the year, but I had been the best she had. She wasn't the best girlfriend ever, but she was the best I had (at the time). Our past relationships weren't great, so we felt amazing together. Neither of us screened effectively or took responsibility for our bullshit. She knew I had anxiety issues. I knew she was a chronic quitter. Despite this, we pushed on because it was easier to outsource love and validation than to take responsibility for our shitbergs.

I knew I was emotionally draining. It wasn't intentional but my self-limiting beliefs told me it was a fucking miracle to be with a woman like her. I was a super needy douchebag. My anxiety came out in a bad way several times though, but, for the most part, I was on top of it. Still, she had a tendency to walk away from anything which got hard. She didn't feel safe or secure. This led to the ultimate demise of our relationship. For context, she never told me she felt unsafe or unheard. I had to learn this after the breakup.

Taking radical responsibility for your part in the breakup is brutal, but it's a necessary evil. Owning your shit will separate your shit from your ex's shit. We take the blame for the failure of the relationship but it's not really anyone's fault. However, if you're going to break up with your breakup truly, you need not pick up what your ex put down.

Your ex was never responsible for your happiness. You were never responsible for your ex's happiness. If someone says, "I'm leaving you because you made me unhappy for the last five years," then why didn't they leave five years ago? You or your ex chose to stay in a situation that no longer worked, and this is on the individual. You can blame your ex for the breakup, but you're responsible for what happens post-breakup.

Exercise:

Conduct an audit of your relationship skills. Look at what you contributed to the breakup. You must be brutally honest with yourself, and it's going to hurt to see your bullshit on paper. However, for you to fix yourself, you must first identify what is wrong.

- Were you ever anxious, avoidant, jealous, or insecure?
- Did you want to win every argument?
- Could you listen to your partner expressing their feelings?
- Did you understand how your partner felt?
- Do you have a habit of shutting down?

When you're done conducting an audit of your relationship skills, also conduct an audit of your ex's relationship skills and ask questions.

- Outside of sex, what did your ex bring to the relationship?
- Were they the avoidant to your anxious attachment style?
- Was their love for you underpinned by respect?
- Did they listen to understand you, over just waiting for their turn to speak?
- Were they able to have healthy distance from you, and maintain a sense of self outside of the relationship?

And so on. Once you've identified their bullshit, I want you to say:

"They are who they are, and it's not my monkey to carry."

Make a promise to yourself that you will fix your bullshit and learn from it.

Case study

It's all your fault: the story of Ryan and Danielle

I first met Ryan in my early 20s. I am now 38, so we've been great friends for a long time. When I first met him, I was a little intimidated. Tall, confident, funny, smart as fuck, good-looking, a few years older than me, and an all-round social butterfly. Essentially, he was everything I was not at the time. I instantly didn't like him because he represented everything I wanted but didn't have the balls to be. After 30 minutes of talking with him, I realised what a genuine and kind human being he was.

We bonded over a mutual love of dark humour and Star Trek. I didn't want to like him because I felt inadequate to him. He could talk to people and pull gorgeous women. His parties were legendary. If you ever wanted to meet new and exciting people, you'd attend one of Ryan's parties. I got with several women over the years at these. I should probably give him some money or something. I eventually got out of my own way and realised he was a good man—a little older, wiser, and someone I could learn much from. To this day, I still go to him when I need help and a verbal slap. He has always told me the truth and calls me on my bullshit. A true friend will stab you in the front, not the back.

At the end of 2014, I was probably at the lowest point I had ever been. The woman I was living with cheated on me, and I kicked her out. I'd never experienced anything like it, which caused me many issues with future girlfriends. I went from having a healthy disposable income to £10 in my account. Still, my mortgage was paid and there was food in the cupboard.

Ryan invited me to a little get-together at his new house in Forest Hill, Southeast London. I remember not wanting to go. However, Ryan was annoyingly good at persuading people to enjoy themselves. I hate and love him at the same time for that. He met me at the train station and asked how I was doing. I said: "What's the fucking point of trying anymore?" I told him it was hard to stay in my flat where my cheating ex lived with me.

Ryan gave me the best advice and it's stuck with me: "Nick, fuck her and fuck your memories in that place. Make new memories and find better women. Women who cheat are always going to cheat. Pick better next time."

Short, compassionate, no bullshit. He made me accountable. He doesn't even remember this chat because he is old, and his party lifestyle wiped away his memory. I know he will read this, and he knows I don't give a monkey's wank either!

Fast forward to 2022 and Ryan is a great guy. In fact, he is too fucking nice. I've seen friends and partners take advantage of him and it fucks me off every time. Credit where credit is due, Ryan cut these people out and instilled stronger boundaries, albeit not always to the best effect.

Ryan started dating Danielle in 2022. Danielle isn't her real name, so for the purposes of this book I named her after Hurricane Danielle. On paper, she was great: smart, funny, and good-looking with two kids in tow. I know the pitfalls of taking on a woman with kids. Most of the time, it is a bad deal for the man because they get all the responsibility and none of the authority.

I gave my unsolicited opinion to Ryan on this, but he was smitten. I shut my mouth and wished him well. A few months in, I was invited to meet Danielle in an East London gallery called *The Approach*. I remember being very impressed. She was a very attractive woman, and she got on well with everyone. I told Ryan she seemed like a keeper, and I was happy for him.

Whenever we had girl trouble, we seemed to end up walking through Victoria Park discussing life and women. Over the years, our ideas and philosophy on relationships certainly have evolved. After many failed attempts at relationships and both of us being fucked over by several women, one starts to abandon the idea of a Disney fairy-tale ending. Just two years prior, we were in Victoria Park having the same conversation; only my relationship was on the rocks. I remember wondering what the fuck I was going to do.

By late 2022, things began to fall apart for Ryan and Danielle. I couldn't help but wonder if Ryan was experiencing the same level of anxiety I had. We grabbed some bagels from the local shop and found a place to sit on the grass. I couldn't help but think how beautiful the park was. Just two years prior, I resented all the couples around me. Two years ago, I wanted the park and everyone in it to be as dark and miserable as I was. But as I sat there talking to one of my best friends, for the first time in a long time, I felt at peace with myself. Ironic!

Ryan told me how Danielle seemed distant and didn't appreciate his efforts. He was trying to take on the role of step-father, supporting her on a charity she had set up and making many home improvements for her. From what Ryan told me, the harder he worked, the less appreciative she would be. The intimacy and affection was drying up quicker than a 90-year-old Nun's vagina. He had told me she would gaslight and stonewall the shit out of him when she didn't get her way. I am not qualified to diagnose conditions, but I started to smell a potential covert narcissist.

The last thing I wanted to do was to turn our chat into a coaching session. After all, he's a good mate, and we've seen and done some crazy shit together. Before giving him my thoughts, I asked how he felt about the situation. He looked at me—defeated. Then he looked at a balding patch of grass, where a thousand people sat before us. Just like that balding patch of grass, Ryan looked just as worn out.

If only that nearby tree could talk, it would have some stories to tell.

Ryan told me how Danielle was passive-aggressive. She would gaslight him and make him feel worthless. He started to question his own integrity and sanity.

By the late year, things were getting worse. After ending things with my new girlfriend, I had just landed back in the UK from the Pacific Northwest in America. I was unhappy, but I couldn't say yes when Ryan asked me if I was upset about wanting to end things. The relief was immense, and I couldn't get on the plane back home fast enough.

After ten hours of jetlag and walking through Heathrow airport, my dad texts me to say he and my mother are in Arrivals. Bless them. I messaged Ryan to exchange war stories on the women in our lives and he told me that he was just about to take off to Europe for a holiday with Danielle and her kids. That was when the shit royally hit the fan. The second he put his foot down and called bullshit, he was asked to leave.

Ryan ordered the wrong hamburger. Stay with me. It will all make sense. Strictly speaking, he didn't order anything wrong, it's one of those places where you order a hamburger and select your own toppings. Ryan let the kid go up to the counter to tell the chef what he would like on the hamburger. The order came out wrong and the kid no longer wanted the hamburger. Danielle started to freak out at Ryan for getting the order wrong. They got into an argument about the restaurant's ordering system, and she started screaming at Ryan. The real issue wasn't the argument itself but how it was fought. Danielle had a well-established record of gaslighting, stonewalling and changing the narrative to fit her confirmation bias.

According to Ryan, the argument got out of hand. The gaslighting and stonewalling continued for the rest of the evening. Ryan texted me, and his tone was just as defeated as on that day in Victoria Park. I advised him to wait until the kids were asleep and discuss it, but I could feel this was terminal.

Ryan explained to Danielle the hamburger situation wasn't anyone's fault. If it had been his fault, he would have ordered another hamburger. Ryan explained how she made him feel. It fell on deaf ears. Danielle replied, "If you didn't make mistakes, I wouldn't get mad. If you stop making me mad with your stupid mistakes, everything would be okay."

Ryan surrendered by this point and knew the relationship was on borrowed time. It's one thing being dressed down in front of her kids and public; it's quite another not to acknowledge how the other party feels.

I remember being very angry on Ryan's behalf then, and I told him he should consider ending the relationship before it worsened. I pointed out it would appear Danielle could not take responsibility for her feelings. Ryan reluctantly agreed, but he had hope. The silly bastard!

The ice queen arrived—no more affection, attention or intimacy. Ryan had just landed back in the UK, and he texted me to say he was feeling very sad and thought it was over. They had broken up already, but no formal declaration had been given. She started acting nice towards Ryan. Not girlfriend nice, more like a stranger in the street nice, or someone I just met on the plane nice. Savage!

There was now a block of ice where her heart used to be. Ryan came to the unfortunate realisation that Danielle's internal issues were too big for him to fix as she was denying them, and it wasn't his job to fix her. He unwillingly filled the role she had hired him to do. She outsourced all her issues and validation to a man because it's too painful to look inward and fix herself. Ryan quickly realised how deep the wounds with Danielle went, and her trauma was now playing out with her kids. Danielle wasn't taking accountability or responsibility for her situation and how she felt. She was using Ryan as an emotional dumping ground. She was happy as long as Ryan was compliant, but he was the bad guy the second he laid down boundaries.

If I were qualified, I would guess Danielle was maybe a narcissist. She certainly met a lot of the criteria. Self-important, charming in front of others who don't know her, love-bombing in the beginning, never said sorry, never took responsibility, never happy with what she had, always sought something new and gaslit the fuck out of people. But I am not qualified, so don't pay attention to anything I say. With that said, one must ask how and why Ryan attracted such a woman, and that was where he needed to focus his self-work.

This was the calm before the storm; everyone knew a breakup was imminent. After a week of her being quiet and not contacting

163

Ryan, he reached out and used this as an opportunity to confront her. She made him wait another week before meeting up and discussing the relationship. This was a dick move, in my opinion.

By this time, I had told Ryan I thought he should end things, but I was almost sure she would end it if Ryan didn't. Sadly, I was right. Ryan got the classic: "It's not you, it's me" speech. He didn't argue and wished her well. He seemed very relieved afterwards.

Three months of no-contact, and she reached out! By this point, Ryan had been doing great. He was disappointed, but he looked happier and healthier all around. I hadn't really noticed how down he had been during the relationship until about two months post-breakup when I met him for a drink, and he just looked happy. But one fateful Friday night, she reached out.

"Would you like to have a drink with me for my birthday? I miss you. Come with me tomorrow. Will you?"

I asked Ryan how he felt about it, and he told me he was at peace and knew they wouldn't work out. Ryan declined the invitation and was met with: "Okay, don't worry."

The breakup wasn't up to Ryan, and he certainly didn't want the breakup to happen. But he took control over how he responded, giving him his power back. Yes, he felt shit for quite some time, but he realised they weren't right for each other. Radical acceptance and responsibility for the situation and how he responded gave him the ultimate power over himself. Read into that what you will, people. For me, this is how a dumpee takes power back and says thanks but no thanks. I've levelled up, and I can do better.

Take home points:

- A disorder of responsibility is needy and unattractive. You can invite someone to love you and to work things out, but you can't make them do it. Trying to negotiate or manipulate your ex to stay validates their decision to leave. Not listening to how they feel and trying to out-logic their feelings says one thing and one thing only. You're not making them feel heard; you're only listening to what you want to hear and not taking responsibility for how you respond to the situation.

- How you respond to your feelings will always determine your happiness or bitterness. Projecting your emotions onto others and blaming the world for your bullshit will only ever keep you stuck.

- We are all fucked up. We all operate from our traumas and worldviews. Therefore, if you were your ex with their bullshit, you would act the same way. Your ex is the hero in their own story. Dumping you made all the sense in the world from their viewpoint. If you don't take responsibility for how you feel, you will never run out of people to blame. If you can take responsibility for everything in your life as if that is precisely what you intended, you will be bulletproof and have a far better outlook.

- Abandon hope and embrace growth. Hope is an approximation created by you. It does not exist. It manifests the belief that we can influence people or events outside our control. The second you understand this and change your mindset, you will be far better off. If you can say to yourself, If scenario A happens, I'm cool with it. If scenario B happens, I'm also cool, and can move forward. Stop hoping and focus on your growth. It's a much better investment of your time.

- The breakup wasn't up to you. Put yourself into your ex-partner's viewpoint and be curious about how they felt about the romantic relationship with you. There was nothing you could've done once they made their decision. There is only choosing how you respond to it.

- Brutal self-reflection and own your shit. It's the only way you will move on and level up. Radical responsibility gets you back.

CHAPTER 7

The Mind Sweep

A round 18 months post-breakup, I realised I used romance to cure my loneliness and always played the rescuer role. The rescuer looks and feels heroic, but they need victims. A rescuer enables the victim; once they have been rescued, they leave. As a formerly anxiously attached man, there was nothing more attractive than an avoidant woman, with a three-month-old baby, living on benefits. I was over it like a homeless person with a bag of chips. I couldn't wait to get the wrapper off and taste the salty goodness.

> "Wanting a relationship to chase away your loneliness is very different from consciously envisaging the qualities and characteristics of the kind of person to whom you want to create a partnership."
>
> — David Emerald, *The Power of TED: The Empowerment Dynamic*

I wasn't creating a partnership with my ex because I never fucking knew how to. I was creating a dynamic where I could swoop in, save the day, be the hero, and have everyone think I was fucking amazing.

And for a time, I was.

I repeated the same tactics as I did with previous girlfriends because that always worked. Well, it would work for three years, and they all fucked off. Only this time, I could rescue the victim and her baby. I was going to look fucking amazing, and I did. I was going to feel needed, and I did. I was curing my loneliness, and that's precisely what happened.

What is it they say about repeating the same shit over and over, then expecting a different result? Something about the definition of madness? Every long-term relationship I had was madness. There was no screening. There was no understanding of the qualities or characteristics of a potential partner because I never understood myself and where my need to rescue came from. Things had to change because this breakup was so fucking painful I started to think that maybe I was the problem. Fuck me, I think the lightbulb just came on.

Viktor Frankl was born in 1905 to a Jewish family in Vienna. He studied philosophy and psychology, and he went on to become a well-renowned psychiatrist. Fast forward to 1938, Hitler, with his mummy and daddy issues (chapter six) became a tyrannical cunt nugget and developed a rather unhealthy obsession with the Jewish people. Frankl, being Jewish and living in Austria, was at the mercy of the Nazi regime. Frankl had the opportunity to go to America before things got bad, but he decided to stay with his parents and the rest of his family.

By 1942, he and his family were arrested by the Nazis and sent to a concentration camp. His father sadly died after six months there, but he, his wife and his mother survived. Two years later, he was sent to Auschwitz along with his wife and mother. His wife was moved to another camp, where she sadly met her untimely demise there, but Frankl did not find out until after the war. His mother was sent to the gas chamber in Auschwitz, and Frankl only narrowly escaped the same fate. 1.3 million people were sent to Auschwitz, and 1.1 million died. Frankl was one of the lucky few to survive.

Forced to endure the inhuman nature of the camps, he was able to find a new mindset and meaning. He held on to his love for his wife; Frankl had to find a way to survive physically and mentally. He was able to take lessons in the suffering that he endured.

> "Everything can be taken from a man but one thing: the last of the human freedoms—to choose one's attitude in any given set of circumstances, to choose one's own way."
>
> — Viktor E. Frankl, *Man's Search for Meaning*

What Frankl found in the concentration camps was a different mindset, a different way to choose how to respond to his suffering. He realised suffering is necessary for meaning and that we are driven to find meaning. He argued later on in his career that to find meaning, we must strike a balance between freedom and responsibility.

My fucking problem is that I was finding meaning by rescuing everyone else at the expense of myself. I found myself stuck with whichever girl liked me enough to stick around. I looked up with puppy-dog eyes like: "Nicky do good?" Ironically, I never had to focus on myself, so they left.

The pain of the breakup, which inspired this book, was the epicentre of my mindset change. I had to ask myself why all my relationships failed within four years. I had to look at the common themes throughout my relationships. There was only one common theme: me. I realised that blaming everyone else never got me anywhere. So, I asked, "What if I took some fucking ownership?" This is when things started to change. I started to break up with the breakup because the pain gave me meaning.

A RELATIONSHIP IS NOT YOUR EVERYTHING

Just like money, love amplifies who people are. If someone poor became rich and turned into a materialistic douchebag, they were always a materialistic douchebag. The money didn't change them, it merely exposed them. If someone falls in love with you and starts treating you with disrespect, they were always toxic.

Love doesn't change anyone; it amplifies their toxicity. The classic: "If you didn't make me angry, I wouldn't treat you this way." Or the frightening: "You made me hit you because you triggered me." This behaviour was always within them.

Shitty behaviour and boundary violations are overlooked because: "We're in love." Two words for you. Fuck! Off! If the relationship is your everything, you'll tolerate a poor excuse for love. After all, if you and your partner can abuse each other, it's fine because it's true love, right? I have another three words for you. Low! Self! Esteem!

Before love, there must be respect and trust. If you're accepting someone else's bullshit values, guess what that means you have? You also have bullshit values. This is where the real work needs to begin for you to unfuck your way out of your breakup.

If all you had with your ex was unresolved emotional issues amplified by love, then you had less than nothing because the foundations were all wrong from the start. However, you made the relationship your everything because you had nothing with yourself. If you had nothing with yourself, what were you bringing to the relationship besides your neediness? If you made the relationship everything, where did you start and your partner stop?

A relationship is bigger than the sum of its parts. It's two individuals with unique ingredients combined to make a recipe. Like a cake, a relationship isn't all just sponge. It's also cream filling and frosting. Although these separate parts come together, you can distinguish every component. The frosting is part of the cake, but you know what's frosting and what's sponge.

I appreciate that this part of the book has entered some weird dimension where cake and frosting are getting dirty. But my point is, just like the cake and frosting, you must bring your uniqueness to the relationship without losing it to the relationship.

If your uniqueness was an act, then the relationship was meaningless. It wasn't real because you never were. The relationship will be doomed if you do not stay true to who you are and what you want.

SEE THE BREAKUP AS A GIFT

I get why seeing one of the most painful events of your life as a gift is a near impossibility. Most people are resistant to a mindset shift. The victim mindset is less painful than the student mindset. Being a student means leaving the devil you know.

- Victim mindset: Blaming others for how they feel, and how they respond to how they feel. This comes with a bachelor's degree in learned helplessness and with a master's degree in self-pity. This can lead to a PhD in low self-esteem.

- Student mindset: Every failure or bad experience is an opportunity to learn and grow. A student doesn't blame anyone for their actions. They accept the situation for what it is. They accept people for who they are. They did what they did and said what they said. It's now my responsibility to not get mad at the situation, but to adapt to the situation and make it work for me.

"What if it was a gift?"

– Dr Robert Glover, *No More Mr Nice Guy*

This could apply to the toxic relationship you have with your breakup. The thing torturing you is the thing you're attached to. Your captor (the breakup) is predictable, so you are familiar with the pain. You know its moods and patterns well enough and if there is one thing humans fucking love, it's homeostasis.

It's comfortable, familiar, predictable and addictive.

But here's the thing: radical acceptance requires a wake-up call. In the introduction to this book, I said: "People only change when the pain of staying the same is no longer an option." There have been times when I've encouraged clients to break no-contact because they had to go and find out. If I can't stop you, I may as well fucking support you. Being rejected twice by the same person or seeing your ex with a new partner might be the pain you need to facilitate radical acceptance.

You can find new meaning and purpose when you're in pain and struggling. Just like Viktor Frankl, the pain becomes the way.

Former world championship boxer Amir Khan found this out the hard way. As an amateur, he won a silver medal for Great Britain in the 2004 Olympics. He was the youngest British boxer to do so. With his newfound stardom, he made his professional debut in July 2005 against David Bailey. 4.4 million viewers tuned in to watch the star, a number that's unheard of for a professional debut.

Between 2005 and 2008, Khan's stock rose sharply. On the 6th of September 2008, Khan was up against a Breidis Prescott. Not much was known about the boxer apart from having good power in both fists and flattening everyone he had been in the ring with. Khan was a massive favourite to win, and what was considered an easy night turned into a nightmare.

55 seconds into round two, Prescott landed a heavy left-right combination to Khan's cranium, flattening the British fighter. Prescott exposed Khan's leaky defence. Everyone was stunned because Prescott wasn't meant to win. This was meant to be a stepping stone to Khan being a world champion.

Arguably, Khan getting knocked out was the best thing that ever happened to him. For most professional athletes, especially boxers, losing is more painful than getting punched in the face. Khan changed trainers and then hired a nutritionist and conditioning coach. He went on to win his next eight fights, beating Andreas Kotelnik for his first world title.

Marcus Maidana was considered one of the division's biggest punchers, and he was far more skilful than Prescott. Khan knocked Maidana down with a crippling body shot but he got back up. Maidana landed weapons-grade plutonium on

Khan's chin, but this time Khan could withstand the onslaught and won the fight.

Heeding the lessons and the gift of being knocked out, Khan became a better boxer and shared the ring with some of the best boxers of his generation. Without the pain and setback from being flattened early on in his career, Khan may never have become as successful as he did. The defeat was painful enough for him not to want to experience that again.

After defeating Khan, Prescott didn't go on to achieve much. He relied too much on the only tool he had, his punch power. His experienced opponents could negate this with ease, and he slowly faded.

Like Prescott, your ex delivered a heavy left-right combination, and it flattened you. To coin a phrase from boxing, it's the punch you don't see that knocks you out. Maybe you saw the breakup coming, or maybe you didn't. Nonetheless, it's not how you get knocked out; it's how you get up and respond. Khan got back up. He allowed himself to feel the pain, but most importantly, he allowed the pain of the loss to teach him exactly the lesson he needed to learn. This led to him becoming a multiple world champion. He adopted the student's mindset. He didn't blame his trainer or that he wasn't feeling great. He took responsibility for his defeat and looked inward to correct his shortcomings in the boxing ring.

Exercise:

Consider for a moment your ex taught you the lesson you needed to learn. What is this lesson, and how would you use it to improve future relationships?

As an example, I would always be attracted to avoidant women who were a flight risk. The lesson for me in this instance is that if I keep choosing avoidant women who are prone to run, stoking my anxiety, then I will always get the same results: me being on the wrong side of a breakup.

THE REBUILD

External validation from family, friends, partners, and colleagues is nice but self-worth, self-esteem, and self-approval are crucial. We need both but most people have an incorrect balance. Most try to get most of their validation from external sources. This is because they never permitted themselves to be okay with who they are.

People very rarely ask: "Why do the people in my life like me?" Most of us think it's because of how impressive we are or what we can offer. In fact, it's more to do with how we make the people around us feel. You can make people feel great by listening and sitting with them.

People say I've made them feel better; all I've done is listen. Before, I felt I had to tell a funny story, make grandiose gestures, and be the fucking hero no one asked for. I thought this because I thought their opinions of me gave me validation.

The thoughts of the people around you do not define you. Don't focus on what others think about you. Rather, focus on how you feel about yourself. After all, who gives a fuck about what someone thinks of you if they don't want to be around you?

If you continue to place too much of your identity and validation on your ex or future partners, you will remain needy as fuck. Neediness is relationship cancer. Most relationship experts say communication (or lack thereof) catalyses a relationship breakdown.

There is something even more fundamental than this. Before having the tools for effective communication, you must permit yourself to be okay with who you are. You must get you right first. If you're not right with yourself, then you're merely shopping for partners who will solve your issues for you, and you're not fussed about the quality of goods you're shopping for.

For me, not being right with yourself comes down to two fundamental things: your ego and dishonesty. You may be asking how low self-esteem can be linked to ego. Here is the thing with ego—it has no balance. It either wants to have the most fantastical life or it wants to have a life that is darker and more depressing than anyone else. This comes back to choosing our metrics for success. If your metric for success is ten million pounds in the bank, and you only have five million, then by that, you have failed. By most other people's metrics, having five million in the bank is a fucking good day at the office.

If you determine your worth only by your relationship status, I have no doubt you will feel like you have the worst life out there because you've chosen a metric that is out of your control. For most people, a breakup is a fucking bad day at the office, but if they have other metrics by which they measure themselves, this can lessen the impact of the breakup and decrease the healing time.

One of the better metrics I adopted through my breakup was to help others. Solving other people's problems helped me find solutions to my own problems. Helping people with their self-esteem boosted my self-esteem. This gave me purpose. As that purpose grew, I started to let go of the value I placed on my relationship with my ex. I would question whether I was a decent person that day or if I helped my friend enough. Even after he was cheated on and diagnosed with cancer two weeks later but recovered and was then diagnosed with a different cancer shortly after (apparently, it's just impossible to kill the bastard and he's doing great now).

Acts of service unlock different parts of you that you never knew existed. It helps you release your ego. When you're serving others, you may find that you don't have to have the best or worst life in the world. You can start a new relationship with yourself rather than having a relationship with your breakup. You can start to write the next chapter of your book and rebuild self-esteem which doesn't hang on to external validation.

Your self-worth will always remain intact regardless of what your ex is doing, provided you upgrade the metrics by which you measure yourself. Your ex-partner's narrative went in a direction you didn't expect or no longer aligned with. However, you must continue writing your book's narrative and chapters because it's yours.

Your story doesn't hinge on one character. All good writers know how to pivot to a new storyline whilst remaining faithful to the zeitgeist of the book (I do not count my shitty writing to be in line with that previous sentence by the way). The zeitgeist of your story existed before your ex came along so, the next chapter you write without them may be shit. You'll find writing much easier once you get the hang of it.

Exercise:

Think of ways you can serve someone that really needs your help—giving one hour of your time a week at a local charity, community centre, library and so on is a great way to serve. Helping others find solutions to their problems can give you a new perspective on how to solve your problems. It also has the happy side effect of meeting people, making friends, and finding purpose, which can help you find a new identity away from your ex and your breakup.

My way was to talk about my breakup, the mistakes I made, what I learned and upload it to YouTube. This evolved into coaching people through their breakups, and now this book that no one will fucking buy. You may choose to do something similar, or you may choose to help at your local dog shelter.

Whatever you choose to do, there is a time to sit in the breakup mud, but there is also a time to act. Helping people through their breakups has been the best way to ground myself in new values. This led to a new purpose, leading me away from measuring myself against my relationship status. This is where you rebuild.

Case Study: The Story of Isabella

After viewing my YouTube channel, Isabella first contacted me in the summer of 2021. She requested a one-to-one coaching session and cancelled at least three times. I wished her well and never expected to hear from her again. I remember being quite disappointed because I hadn't been coaching long and I needed every client I could get. She later reached out and confirmed a session with me.

From the start, Isabella had no sense of boundaries or vulnerability and she was displaying signs of a fearful avoidant. As I dug deeper into her relationship history, I found she had a string of high-octane flings or would date men with low self-esteem. She was operating in extremes. The high-octane flings were with men that had celebrity lifestyles, and seemingly didn't care were exciting but lacked security. The low self-esteem men were dull, boring and didn't stimulate her.

She was with a long-term partner whom she had no romantic love for. They didn't have anything in common. He was dull, insecure, and passive-aggressive. Pretty much everything Isabella and most women hate in men. Isabella wanted to stick this one out as she thought it was the right thing to do. The crazy nomad party lifestyle with a string of failed flings and half relationships had left her wanting something more long-term, safe, and settled.

Unbeknownst to Isabella, she got what she wanted. Boring with a side of passionless sex. This reflected Isabella's self-worth and self-esteem. She'd never taken responsibility for herself or validated her emotions. Hence, chasing high after high. She sought relief and validation in all the wrong places.

One fateful day, Isabella was introduced to the narcissist. He was charming, charismatic, and adventurous—everything her current boyfriend wasn't. She thought she had found salvation and began an affair.

Isabella had buried her trauma and outsourced it to men to take care of it for her. As a beautiful young woman, she had no shortage of potential suitors, but she would always choose the wrong type of man because her trauma told her it's all she was good for.

When we lack self-awareness, we repeat the same patterns. This is exactly what happened. Isabella hadn't spent any real time being single and when she was, she moved place to place, job to job, seeking relief.

To quote Dr Robert Glover, "The opposite of crazy is still crazy."

Isabella was about to get all the crazy she could handle.

So, this narcissist ended up having mummy issues, childhood trauma, and a wife who left him for his brother. I knew this would be a challenge for Isabella. My only thought at the time was: "Why the fuck were you with someone like this?"

Isabella told me he was the first guy she truly loved. But she had been love-bombed by him from the start. Unbeknownst to her, underneath the hot, sexy, adventurous exterior lay a heavy drinker, drug addict, and a bad-tempered emotional vampire who had to be the centre of attention. He wasn't satisfied with being the hero of his own story; he also had to make himself the hero of everyone else's story.

Isabella could've made the healthier decision of ending the boring relationship and figuring out her own bullshit. Instead, she was in league with a dark knight she couldn't control.

Don't get me wrong, everything was great for the first six months, which is the average time in most relationships. Most people can keep the crazy under control for three to six months, and then the crazy takes over. After a hot honeymoon period, Isabella's appeal for the narc wore off. The more unsatisfied he became, the more Isabella sacrificed to appease him.

They say if you show a dog love, it will love you back a hundred-fold, but if you show it violence, it will mimic this as well until it literally bites the hand that feeds it. Just like the dog, Isabella started to mimic the traits of her master, matching his level of crazy.

For the first time in her romantic life, Isabella was vulnerable with a man who depended on women with low self-esteem to tolerate him. A narc who needed someone who couldn't say no and Isabella needed someone she could fix.

Isabella chose to ignore his red flags. After 18 months, the narc ended the relationship and was in a new relationship within three weeks. I explained to Isabella that he merely found a new source to suck dry and she should focus on healing her trauma.

Discarded and with nowhere to go, she had to move back in with her parents (which she saw as some personal humiliation). I tried to explain to Isabella that I'd rather move back in with my parents than be with an emotional vampire for the rest of my life. I went on to say she had been given a gift.

Isabella was trying to find salvation in a constant string of highs. Still, these quickly became normal, leading her to find ever more solutions to her trauma and unhappiness. Seeking happiness or seeing happiness as a destination is a form of avoidance. Seeking new highs and thrills is avoidance in every sense of the word. Isabella had been avoiding her emotions through drink, drugs, job hopping, a party lifestyle and boyfriends just as fucked up as her.

This may seem like a brutal account but it's the truth. My job as a coach, content creator, and author (I write narcissistically), is to give the truth, no matter how raw it may be.

This has been a particularly hard part of the book to write because Isabella is a close friend of mine. In fact, I can't imagine my life without her in it now. She drives me fucking crazy sometimes with her glass-half-empty worldview and self-detrimental comments, but she has a good heart, soul and I can say she is someone I truly care about. She is doing much better for herself by rebuilding her life with an exciting career change.

Despite this being a crushing breakup for Isabella, she realised her ex taught her a lesson she needed to learn. This life changing lesson may surprise you. It certainly surprised Isabella. She realised she is responsible for the men she lies with. She learned that an amazing connection isn't an indicator of compatibility or success. She mistook highs for happiness. She realised the men she chooses reflect who she is, and therefore she has to look inward to find her power, healing and, most importantly, herself.

Isabella projected her anger onto her ex for a long time. However, over the course of her coaching sessions with me and ongoing friendship, she slowly stopped blaming him. Yes, he did a lot of fucked up shit, and I by no means excuse his behaviour. Yet, for Isabella to heed the lesson she was being taught, she had to accept a few truths: her ex is who he is, he did what he did and he said what he said. That wasn't a reflection of Isabella. He has his traumas, his worldview, and his baggage. He is just as broken as anyone else and needs help. Forgiving him isn't about excusing his actions but letting go of their weight.

Forgiving him removed his hold over her and she became emotionally unencumbered.

CHAPTER 8

Jigsaw

Comedian Daniel Sloss hilariously explains why most relationships fail in his Netflix special, *Jigsaw*. In fact, it is so good I will rip it off unashamedly.

Life is a giant jigsaw, but we've lost the box and don't know what the picture looks like. What do we do if we have lost the box? We start with the four corners of the jigsaw. The four corners of our life jigsaw are family, friends, hobbies/interests, work/career. We spend our whole lives building these four corners. Sometimes, we have to move them around or focus more on one corner that needs our attention. Friends come and go, hobbies change, we get promoted, and sometimes we choose not to see certain family members anymore.

What about the centre of the jigsaw?

That is the relationship and partner piece.

We spend a significant amount of time and resources searching for that one last piece at the expense of our four corners. So much time is spent in the centre, our four corners crumble. We fall apart.

Undeterred with our four corners crumbling, we look for that centrepiece. We become so focused on trying to live a future that does not exist that we stop living the life we have now. So when we find someone who validates us and makes us feel amazing, we feel limerence—that cloud nine Disney-level love.

There is just one problem. We're not screening this partner properly. We're not taking the time to assess our compatibility. We've neglected ourselves so severely in pursuing "the one" that we're employing our romantic partners to be an entire village.

The problem is your partner is their own jigsaw. They've spent their whole lives moving pieces to form the puzzle of their existence. In all likelihood, this is not compatible with your jigsaw.

Nonetheless, we take their jigsaw piece and ram it into the centre of our own, trying to make it fit. We can flip it and turn it upside down, hoping it will fit. Our four corners are so weakened by neglect and trauma we need their centrepiece to fix it.

Somehow, we make it fit and are okay for a year, two, five, ten, and beyond.

One day, you'll discover the person in the middle of our jigsaw doesn't fit and never did. You would've figured this out sooner if you screened them for compatibility. Maybe you want kids, and they don't. Maybe they love travelling, and you're a homebody. Maybe you're a leftist, and they're all for the right. Maybe they love a cuddle, and you like long conversations. But none of this mattered earlier because you were in love, living a fantasy, sacrificing values, boundaries, and yourself for a happily-ever-after. The relationship with yourself is so poor you'd gladly sacrifice your sense of self to cling to a shit relationship over having no relationship.

Five years later, you still want what you want, and they want what they want. You're heading in different directions. Your jigsaw pieces still don't fit and are forcefully wedged together. Values, maturity, political views, religious views and so on. These all make up your jigsaw. You must make the right jigsaw piece to fit your jigsaw. A relationship can soothe your emotional wounds for a short amount of time, but the mask will slip one day and the real you will shine through. The romanticised fantasy of you is just that–a fantasy.

A healthy, committed, happy relationship where both people's needs are met will enhance your happiness, but it is not and never should be your entire happiness. I promise you this. Being in a relationship with someone who isn't compatible will make you feel lonelier than when you were actually alone.

Build your four corners with balance. I see too many people, women more than men, hyper-focused on work/career at the expense of the rest of their jigsaw. Conversely, I see too many people, ironically men more than women, needing to focus more on work. They are focused on friends, hobbies, and interests. I also see women in their 30s and 40s devastated they don't have children yet because they spent too much time focused on their careers, partying, or convinced they don't need a man. I see men devastated by divorce who can't get another date because they're immature. I see men and women picking the wrong jigsaw piece simply because they're lonely.

Too many people need to work on themselves and rely on others to complete them.

Love is never enough! Before romantic love, there needs to be a foundation of self-validation, self-respect, self-esteem and, above all fucking else, vulnerability! But no, rather than taking responsibility for our emotional well-being, we blame others. Instead of recognising the challenges unique to both sexes and to us, we say shit like: "All women are gold diggers" or "All men are cheaters".

Allow me to translate:

Nobody wants to admit they are the problem because then you'd have to self-reflect. We need to stop blaming each other. This spreads hate and resentment. This will be the hippiest fucking thing you'll ever hear me say:

The only thing that can defeat hate is empathy and patience.

We love to point the finger because it is opposite our reflection. It's someone else. It's *them*. What you hate about your partner is likely what you hate about yourself. This is called: *projection*. We project because we don't want to look inside ourselves.

Projecting emotions doesn't help you understand your actions. Instead of reflecting on your feelings or actions, you hold others accountable. As a result, you do not solve your problems, you create more. As you project your issues, you prevent yourself from understanding others.

You locked that wound in a box long ago and put it under your bed. Out of sight out of mind. That's the side of you that needs the most work. You can either leave that part of you under the bed, or you can take that part of you that is in the most amount of pain and give it the love and care it needs. That is the part causing your relationships to fail and your jigsaw to crumble. Build your jigsaw well and search for the last piece that fits. Maintain your jigsaw by moving things around and caring for the needed parts.

You are so occupied with attributing your emotions that you hope others feel what you have. You are making your experiences their own, and thus, you fail to see that other people are not entirely similar to you and have a life of their own.

As mentioned, projecting behaviour or emotions might be obscure to spot. Here are some examples:

1. Expecting the worst

    Relationships are built around positivity. However, if you expect things to go wrong, this is a bad habit. Do you expect your partner to cheat on you? They might not be displaying signs of treachery, but in your mind, you are building a perception that they will betray you.

2. Changing the story

    Projecting often leads to victimisation. Sometimes, you might even change the story to make it work in your favour. For example, people who cheat or leave can sometimes blame their actions on their partners. Some even go to extremes to torture their partners or put them in harm's way.

3. Overreacting

    If you overreact, things can quickly be blown out of proportion. If you feel like what the other person did is a bigger deal than it was, this can be harmful. You might become aggressive towards your partner, and you only feel regret when you calm down.

4. Selective hearing

Because of your guilt, you're likely to become less open-minded. You might start dismissing your partner's emotions by projecting your own first. In this case, the argument will appear one-sided since you mask your actions' reality.

5. Making unfair comparisons

If you project your emotions, you can overreact and create unfair conclusions or comparisons due to unresolved trauma. For example, maybe your partner went to the shop and got a cake for themselves, but when they got home, you were upset they didn't think of you, and you thought it was because they don't care about you at all.

THE BIGGEST RED FLAG IS ALWAYS YOURSELF

Never take advice from a starving person trying to sell you something.

Allow me to translate:

A starving person might be desperate enough to sell shoes to a snake. They will convince the snake it needs shoes and that shoes will be the answer to all its problems. Despite the snake living just fine without shoes, the starving person convinces the snake it needs them. Someone who isn't starving does not need to make such a fraudulent sale. They are okay waiting for the right person who wants to buy shoes. This is because they have invested time and energy into their values.

I will go further and say: Never date an emotionally starved person. They will sell a version of themselves that is not true.

And by person, I mean you. You will always be your own red flag. Until you fix your red flags, you will attract red flags.

Like a McDonalds Big Mac, you make yourself look fucking amazing on the dating menu. You post your six best pictures, talk about your hobbies, how you volunteer and what a great person you are. Only this is a load of shit. Like the Big Mac, when someone opens the box, it is different from what was advertised on the menu. What they find is a miserable hamburger.

Not to say you look like stringy brown lettuce or are miserable, but you're not what you're advertising. When your ex looked deeper, they found an emotionally starved individual.

You sold shoes to a snake.

I swear I'm a nice guy in real life. It's just... writing a book allows you to be a dick.

To have a well-balanced and happy relationship with another, you must have a well-balanced and happy relationship with yourself. This is old news. But why work on yourself when you can outsource from someone else? They will work on you so they, too, can avoid working on themselves. How cancerous is that? Having shitty relationships with shitty people is nothing more than avoiding yourself. Therefore, I think sometimes rather than asking, "Why did my ex leave me?" we should be asking, "Why did I choose their bullshit, and why did they choose my bullshit?"

Exercise:

What are your fucked up red flags?

Brutal honesty will set you free. Do you always fall for the bad boy gangsters or the damsel in distress with daddy issues? Do you always date anxious people, avoidants, and emotionally unavailable people? Is your idea of love shouting and screaming at each other because that's how your parents treated each other, and you? Do you always put everyone's needs above yours because you have shitty boundaries?

After you've compiled your list, ask yourself why these red flags exist within you. You must be brutally honest. If you're someone solely attracted to bad boys, ask yourself why. Is it familiar to you because your mother dated the same kind of men, and that's what your blueprint of love looks like?

If you're attracted to the damsel in distress, maybe it's because you desire validation because no one rescued you. If all your relationships were nothing more than shouting, examine whether your idea of romance was influenced by seeing your parents scream at each other.

With brutal honesty comes brutal responsibility. How do you go from being attracted to the bad boy, to being attracted to someone who obeys the law? How can you stop rescuing the damsel in distress and start saving yourself?

How do you identify your own red flags? There are several ways this can be achieved which I'll go into, but my personal favorite is to get yourself a Sagi.

What the fuck is a Sagi, I hear you ask?

Great question.

Sagi was a former client of mine who became a great friend and advisor. Sagi was about as subtle as a grenade. He is a former airline pilot, and he wouldn't allow me to submit the Qantas flight story from Chapter Four until every detail was accurate. The first time I gave it to him for feedback it was fucking brutal. But this is exactly why I value his friendship. Seeking constant feedback from someone like Sagi keeps my feet on the ground and my red flags in check. Keeping honest people in my life that do not allow me to exist in an echo chamber is my preferred way to identify red flags.

Just fucking ask, "Hey was I being a dick here, or was I right to call bullshit on my partner's reaction?"

I appreciate you may not have such people in your life.

If you don't have a Sagi, look back on your relationship history and look for your common red flags. Did you always go for partners that smothered you and slowly eroded your independence? Do you always go for someone that is emotionally unavailable, despite you needing and enjoying an attentive and emotionally available partner? Do you constantly choose people that do not align with your lifestyle? They like to drink but you're teetotal.

If choosing the wrong jigsaw piece only happened the once, put it down to experience and move on. If you keep choosing incorrectly, then that is your red flag and not the person you chose.

This next one is fucking brutal so strap in. Look for the red flags in your parents, because that is our first blueprint of what a relationship looks like. We all pick up at least some traits from our parents. I got my past anxiousness from my mother, and my past stubbornness and need to win every argument from my dad. Put a stubborn anxious person in a room with an avoidant and watch the fucking fireworks. Pretty much every breakup I had followed that script. Who's the red flag here? The women or my choice of women? If you're getting the same outcome from every relationship you're in, then it's not them, it is you that is waving red flags.

Always remember: to have the jigsaw you want; you must know what your four corners look like. Your jigsaw is a reflection; therefore, if the portrait is jumbled, rammed together, and incomplete, you will be so too.

PURPOSE

Since my breakup I have dated a ton. Most were flings or friends with benefits, but I was semi-serious with three women. By 'semi-serious' I mean it was more than just sex and we were dating. None of them worked out. In each case, I was the dumper. They were all lovely but not for me. When I knew things wouldn't work out, my anxiety increased. There was a war between the old me and the new me. The old me wanted to avoid being alone and thus cover up any chance of a breakup.

But the new me knew I wasn't happy.

I could have easily stayed. She was emotionally unavailable and traumatised by a previous relationship, and I was looking for someone to save. If I were to save her, I would not focus on my own pain. She was perfect for the old me. But I was learning. I spotted her red flags early because I was working on mine. Unlike before, I found ways to validate myself: YouTube, content writing, and coaching.

I had a purpose beyond her.

Finding purpose is in the foundation of your being. Without a purpose building you up, you will find purpose in your partners. They become everything because you are your nothing. This is the very definition of self-abandonment. So, finding a purpose can be the path back to reconnecting and healing.

What does purpose look like?

Your life purpose consists of the central motivating aims of your life—the reasons you get out of bed.

Purpose guides life decisions, influences behaviour, shapes goals, offers direction, and creates meaning. For some, purpose is connected to their vocation—meaningful, satisfying work. For others, purpose lies in their responsibilities to their family or friends. Others seek meaning through spirituality or religious beliefs. Some find their purpose clearly expressed in all these aspects of life.

Purpose is unique to everyone. What you identify as your path may be different from others. What's more, your purpose can actually shift and change in response to the evolving values and priorities of your own experiences.

Questions that may come up when you reflect upon your life purpose are:

- *Who am I?*
- *Where do I belong?*
- *When do I feel fulfilled?*

When you have purpose, you will hold yourself in higher esteem and to a higher standard. You will seek the same in your romantic partners when you hold yourself to a higher standard based on better values. It seems overly simplistic in theory, and that's because it is. The problem most people have is implementation because it's easier to employ a partner to make everything better for you.

If you have no other reason to seek out a partner other than soothing your loneliness and to validate you, maybe you lack purpose in your life. If you lack purpose, you're not growing. There is only one destination: a breakup.

> "If you're not growing, you're dying."
>
> — Tony Robbins

Misery always wants company. When two people without purpose find each other, they think they have a purpose. They shoehorn themselves into each other's jigsaw, despite knowing it's a poor fit. I am not saying a romantic partner cannot make up some of your purpose, but most of your purpose should be focused on yourself.

If you want a sexy as fuck jigsaw rather than a miserable one, you must adopt a growth mindset. A growth mindset is choosing the path of most resistance in this context. It's choosing to own the shit you're shit at. It is choosing to be better at the shit you're (currently) shit at.

Choosing you is an investment in your future and, for me, this facilitates the best opportunities of choosing a partner that matches your energy and crazy. Your willingness to grow, challenge yourself, and be better than yesterday is sexy as fuck. Your jigsaw will be sexy as fuck, and you will attract just as sexy as fuck romantic partners.

Take home points:

- Take time to build your jigsaw. Too many are eager to live their future, they are prepared to sacrifice the life they are living now. To sacrifice the life you are living today is to abandon yourself for a future that does not yet exist.

- Fix your red flags. This is what ultimately led to your breakup. Maybe you loved too much or not enough. Your red flags reflect the red flags you attract in a partner and vice versa. If you're a walking red flag, guess what your ex and future partners will be.

- Find your purpose before finding a romantic partner. If you find a partner beforehand, your partner becomes your purpose. If your partner is your only purpose, the relationship will kill itself quicker than a baby with a razor blade. It will also make the breakups a lot harder than necessary because you have no fucking clue who you are.

Case study

The best breakup movie ever: *Forgetting Sarah Marshall*

Forgetting Sarah Marshall is the best breakup movie of all time for me. It's a story of an ugly breakup that ends pretty well. It's authentic to what an actual breakup process looks like. It diverts from the typical happily-ever-after bullshit.

Peter is a lazy, overweight, and complacent musician. His girlfriend, Sarah, is a successful actress supporting Peter financially and emotionally. Peter made Sarah his whole world. In doing so, he lost his purpose. He spends his days procrastinating, eating cereal from a dog bowl and doing bad impressions from *Lord Of The Rings*. I appreciate that this isn't particularly interesting, but one must set the scene for the breakup and his recovery journey.

Get off my back, you judgemental fuck! Just kidding, I love you, really.

Sarah is living her life and bossing her career. She's evolving, levelling up, and leaving Peter behind. He is not evolving with her. This is relationship cancer. It's not what Sarah signed up for. Love is not unconditional, despite what a lot of people think. Romantic love is very much conditional, from physical attraction to emotional maturity. She started dating Peter based on conditions he is no longer fulfilling, and now she's about ready to throw in the towel.

The Breakup:

Often, the dumpee senses a change. Peter knows Sarah is about to dump him. He bargains with Sarah as she says: "We've been growing apart, and we're living different lives." Rather than listening to Sarah, he accuses her of cheating. This pushes Sarah away, and she leaves.

You see, Sarah didn't just wake up and decide to dump Peter. The relationship stopped working (for her) a long time ago, but she stayed, hoping Peter would get his shit together. Sadly, Peter never did. She no longer sees a future with Peter. It stopped being about Peter long ago and is now about Sarah's aspirations for her future.

As breakups go, this was fucking brutal. The whole thing took two minutes and 22 seconds. Peter had gone from feeling safe in a relationship to being dumped to finding out Sarah was cheating on him. The poor guy didn't even have time to get dressed, and Sarah was out of the door before you could say: Sarah Marshall.

The Anger Phase:

"I thought I was fine, and I am not. I am not fine at all."

Everything reminds Peter of Sarah. To rub salt in the wound, Peter works with Sarah and creates the music for her TV show, meaning he has to see her every day. He can't focus on work and is almost convinced she is banging every man on set. A lesson to everyone reading, don't shit where you eat. I have made the mistake of dating women who I work with, and it's a clusterfuck when it goes wrong. If you think you're struggling with no-contact, try no-contact when you have to see the fucker every day.

Sadly, Peter is still not getting it. His brother tells him he always thought Sarah was a bitch, and so did everyone else. Peter refuses to accept what his brother is saying because he has Sarah so high up on a pedestal that he doesn't know his arsehole from his elbow.

You might think your ex was the best thing since sliced bread, but billions of people out there probably would never hold your ex in high esteem. To most other people, what you think is exceptional is mediocre at best, so take your ex down from the pedestal. They're average humans living on an average planet, circling an average star. Their existence is but one second of the life of the universe.

The Doing Crazy Shit and Stalking Phase:

Arguably, it's one of the best parts of a breakup. My crazy phase took me to countries, on adventures, to women and new people.

Peter jets off to Hawaii because Sarah mentioned she always wanted to go there. But oh no! Sarah is staying at the same hotel with her new boyfriend. Undeterred, Peter is determined to have a good time when he's not crying. The hotel receptionist, Rachel (played by Mila Kunis) (I so would), sees the dynamic between Peter and Sarah. Putting two and two together, she realises Peter has been screwed over. She gives Peter the best suite in the hotel to make him look a little better in front of Sarah.

But it's not all easy on the dumper's side. Sarah's new boyfriend is a free-spirited rock star who isn't into monogamy. He's the opposite of who Sarah wants to be with. She hasn't taken responsibility for her feelings and is outsourcing them to her new partner.

Peter commits the cardinal sin when discovering an ex is with someone new. He stalks her.

To stick the knife in even further, Peter is surrounded by newlyweds and couples, reminding him how lonely he is. This is called the Baader-Meinhof phenomenon; the frequency illusion. Our brains have selective attention when we're excited and, in Peter's case, if you're hugely distressed about something, you start seeing that thing everywhere you go. I am sure most of you noticed way more happy couples in the first three months of your breakup.

Another example is if you're looking to buy a new iPhone or Tesla Model S, you start to see that item everywhere you go, or so you think. In reality, when a significant event in your life has occurred, or something is trending in your mind, it dominates your consciousness, creating a bias and making you hyper-observant for that thing. You're not actually seeing more Teslas on the road or happy couples everywhere you go, you're just hyper-aware of them. Our brain seems to love fucking us with every opportunity it gets.

It's at this point we see Peter call Sarah out on her bullshit. He tells her not everything is about her. She is visibly uncomfortable because this is the first time Peter says no to her.

The rock bottom phase:

This phase is different for everyone. Peter goes through an excessive period where you talk about your ex to anyone who will listen.

Then…

Peter starts to try new things. For the first time in months, he feels better. Peter is starting to accept it's over, but his anxiety and his need for external validation is still fucking with him. He's still in the mud, but his new friends aren't letting him do this alone, and he's realised one crucial thing: he can't fall any lower, so he may as well start climbing.

The re-emerging phase:

Finally! Peter finds his daddy's bags and remembers what they are for. He asks Rachel, the receptionist, out.

Here's a little tip from Dr Robert Glover's book Dating Essentials For Men: Two hours, coffee shop, vibe check, that's it! Dating is an expensive hobby.

Game changer! Arrange the fucking date and get to it.

Given how many dates I've been on over the last three years, I quickly realised I needed to streamline my work. Firstly, the demands on my time are extreme, so I don't want to waste too much time on women I don't want a second date with, hence only two hours for the first date. Secondly, you don't want to drop £100 to £200 every first date, so keep it local and casual. A trendy coffee shop is a great spot to see if you vibe. If you do, arrange a second date at a nice bar in the evening. If you're not feeling it, thank them for their time and continue your life.

Peter is doing things he has never done with people he would usually never hang out with. That is the great thing about breakups. They can push you into dimensions you never knew existed. His real ambition is to write his own musicals.

Rachel calls him out on his bullshit and tells him if he hates his job to fucking change it. Peter's ego takes a knock here, but he gets over it and realises he's needed a verbal slap for quite some time.

Rachel shows him what a different partner can bring to the table, and at this point, he starts to forget Sarah Marshall. Peter realises what he has been missing and how shitty his relationship really was.

Sarah did him a solid. It is starting to look like this was the best thing to ever happen to Peter. It's just a shame it took this level of trauma for him to realise it.

And it all starts to go wrong for Sarah:

The walls of reality rapidly close in on Sarah, and she quickly realises she's not as important as she thinks. Her TV show is cancelled, and her rock star boyfriend is on tour for 18 months. Sarah doesn't react well to this because she no longer controls the situation.

Sarah tells Aldous she can't go on tour with him because she is a working actress, and in what I think is the most subtle but brutal line of the film, he responds with, "Not anymore. You're an unemployed actress." Sarah is very much getting a problematic lesson on external validation. She depended on her job and fame for her validation, and if she had stayed with Peter, he would've been there to validate and console her.

The genuine Sarah reveals herself and admits to Peter that she is scared she will be forgotten if she steps out of the spotlight. This is where the mother of all reversals happens because Peter validates her concerns while making her laugh, and Sarah realises she made a huge mistake leaving him. For the first time, Peter is showing confidence and finding his centre, which is super sexy and attractive. He was able to sit there with his cheating ex-girlfriend and listen to her bullshit without losing control. Legend!

Peter has a flashback where he plays a song for Sarah from the musical he is writing. He is quickly reminded of what a shitty girlfriend she had been because she wasn't showing interest in his projects, where he would support hers unconditionally. At this point, Peter is getting himself back and re-emerging whilst the pendulum of power of the breakup just swung to him. He's heading towards relief and renewal, whereas the breakup just became very real for Sarah, as she no longer has a job and her rock star boyfriend isn't what she wants him to be. One might say that is poetic justice.

Peter stands on the edge of a cliff with Rachel. Next to him is a beautiful new woman who wants his company and shows Peter what a real connection could be. In front of him is the final last jump he must take and somehow learn how to fly on the way down. The precipice before him represents his fear and angst about forgetting Sarah Marshall. All he has to do is jump! Rachel, played by Mila Kunis (I so would), leaps off into the sea below, inviting Peter to join her. Peter is still questioning if he should stay on top of the cliff with Sarah and the devil he knows or take a leap and explore new adventures with Rachel.

There's one thing I can tell you from personal experience with decisions like this. Indecision is a slow death; therefore, the only thing worse than making a wrong decision is not making a decision. When you're faced with a leap of faith, just fucking take it. You may land hard, but at least you tried and moved on from where you were.

The final boss:

Peter and Sarah have it out. Peter confronts her about cheating on him. Sarah has zero excuse for cheating, and she admits it's nothing Peter did and more about what he didn't do. She got tired of taking care of him when he stopped taking care of himself.

Nothing is more unattractive than someone sacrificing themselves like that in a relationship. A relationship is two people putting 50% in and using the remaining 50% on themselves. To her credit, I do believe Sarah wanted things to work, but she was the victim of her own creation.

Things between Sarah and Aldous start to spiral, and she very quickly realises they are all wrong for each other. Peter and Rachel are functioning well and taking each day as it comes, enjoying each other's company without trying to fix each other.

For the first time in Sarah's life, she is not in control, and the world no longer revolves around her. She ousted her white knight; the dark night saw through her bullshit, and she's fading from the spotlight.

Get that girl a napkin because she just got served.

Meanwhile, Peter and Rachel are getting closer all the time, and Peter is discovering that there may be a better woman for him in Rachel. Rachel gets excited by Peter's passion for wanting to write a musical. She has no interest in the arts, but she's excited that he has interests, and there is nothing more attractive to a woman than a man on his purpose.

Peter gets excited over how Rachel is more adventurous than he is and loves doing the little things in life, which brings out an adventurous side of him that he never knew existed.

When Sarah first met Aldous, he was the shiny new toy. He was intoxicating and exciting; she fell in love with a reflection of herself. He is a self-obsessed egomaniac, only his ego is bigger.

Peter finds himself consoling Sarah. He still cares about her, but the romance boat sunk when she decided to cheat. Sarah is laying it out to Peter, calling Aldous a prick. I agree, Aldous is a prick, but he's my kind of prick. We know exactly where we stand with him, and he will tell us how it is. Sarah admits to not being over Peter and that she royally fucked up.

But, is it true, or just a reflex action of losing her TV show and Aldous?

I think Peter quickly realises he is the backup plan and knows his worth now. He has vastly outgrown Sarah morally and emotionally and sees her for what she really is—a scared little girl who cannot validate herself without a man or fame.

"Maybe the problem is that you broke my heart into a million pieces and so my cock doesn't want to be around you anymore! Okay? EVER! Because you know what I just realised? You're the goddamn devil!"

Peter is by no means perfect, and he has his issues. But throughout this journey, we have discovered one monumental life lesson. If your current version no longer works and serves you, that version of you must die for a new version to be born!

The problem is that the old version is part of our identity and our story. It will go down screaming and kicking; sometimes, it will try to dig out of the underworld. How do I know that? Because my old version could never have written this book, I stand here with you today, telling you that you will be okay. However, there will be a lot of pain on the path to your recovery, just like Peter had to go through. When Peter jumped off the cliff with Rachel, the old version of him died, but what emerged was a new Peter with self-love, boundaries and the knowledge that he can do better.

And that, my friends, is why *Forgetting Sarah Marshall* is the greatest breakup movie ever.

CHAPTER 9

The Happy Now

WHERE AM I NOW?

For the book's final chapter, I wanted to share life-changing lessons I've learned during and after my breakup. I wanted to share what happened when I recovered.

You see, I had to die to write this book. I had to die to be able to tell you taking responsibility for yourself is the ultimate form of self-love. I had to die to tell you I know you will be okay because I am okay. Everyone I have coached through their breakup is okay. I didn't die literally, but the version of me that my ex dumped died. Metaphorically, my identity died for my new identity to grow.

We are all the heroes of our stories. Just like every hero story, we need a villain. I will bet my mortgage you cast your ex in *that* role. Come now, don't bullshit me. It's okay if you did. As imperfect humans, we want to protect our identities and outsource responsibility. Sadly, this cannot continue to recover. The villain in your story isn't your ex; it's you. The villain is doubt, self-hate, and self-deprecation. Yet, the fucked up thing is we need a villain to have a great story. We need to villainise something to facilitate growth and change. By villainising our pain and struggle, we localise the source of failure we need to compare success and happiness.

We're just lazy, dopamine-addicted Homo sapiens. But we don't have to be slaves to our hormones and trauma. If I had continued to do so, I never would've reached my full potential. So, understand that you do not have a hero story if you do not acknowledge yourself as a limited-belief monkey who needs to amend their values.

Writing this book has been a journey. I've had to revisit uncomfortable memories, realise uncomfortable truths, conquer my limited-belief monkey, and examine my traumas. When I started to write this book, it wasn't a book, it was YouTube content. When I just kept writing, I thought fuck it, I might as well keep going and see what happens. I even thought I was writing the best breakup book ever!

No.

The best advice any writer needs is: write the book you want to read. So, I wrote the book I would've needed after my breakups. It is a shame I had to navigate the post-breakup sphere without the exact words I needed, but now I give all my knowledge to you.

This book and my YouTube content focus on the power of taking responsibility. Of course, it's not an original concept; look at all of the references I've made to other authors, for fuck's sake!

Yet I knew I had to put my spin on it.

My spin is that the breakup isn't about you. The breakup is your ex's decision. They never set out to hurt you, and they're not out to get you. Everything they do, say and think reflects their traumas and experiences. How they feel is always okay. But you also have a right to your feelings, and once someone makes you feel shunned, abandoned, or hurt, it is also okay to take a step back.

Self-preservation can be viewed as narcissistic, as self-preservation is the instinct to live and preserve one's life. Narcissistic self-preservation is the instinct to live and preserve one's life in a self-centred and egotistical way. This self-preservation type is often motivated by a fear of losing what one has. Narcissistic self-preservation can lead to selfishness and self-destruction. But to keep us safe, self-preservation can stop us from evolving. When our identities are challenged, we will pretty much die to protect them.

I have news for you. Everyone is imperfect. We are constantly challenged because we're always growing and evolving. You will die one day. After a while, no one will ever know you existed (unless you're famous). So, will you sit there wondering what your ex is doing and hoping they will return? Or will you get up off your knees, take responsibility for how you feel and stop trying to lose and start trying to win?

Life isn't about trying not to die but trying to live well.

I've come to learn people only change when staying the same is no longer an option. Your ex didn't magically change who they were, nor did they wake up one day and decide to dump you. It is a little like this:

Time + Repetition + Emotion = Change

Therefore, if you didn't recognise the change in emotions over time, then that's a failure on your part. If you failed to recognise your partner's growth and stayed exactly where you were, that is on you!

The good news is it's never too late to evolve and readjust. Self-love is, for me, the most painful and brutal thing we can do for ourselves. It's putting yourself first and fucking off anyone who isn't bringing anything to the table. This means we might be lonely for a while but try being in a relationship that isn't going anywhere or realising you've been with the wrong person for ten years. That is the loneliest place in the world.

There is good and bad pain, just like good and bad debt. Here's a cheeky quote from one of my favourite films:

> "Bad debt is having a credit card so you can work jobs you hate to pay for the shit you don't need."
>
> – *Fight Club*

Good debt is saving for a deposit to get a mortgage. Bad debt is renting a flat with the wrong person and living with them for a fucking long time. Good pain is leaving that persona and giving up the rented flat. Bad pain is staying in that relationship. Choose good pain. Good pain is you breaking up with your breakup.

So, why is good pain important?

It hurts, but you'll be happy about it in the end.

FINDING HAPPINESS IN ALL THE WRONG PLACES

I have enjoyed coaching people worldwide through dating, breakups, and relationships. It's a pleasure to help people. One thing all of them have in common is: "Nick, I just want to be happy—I want to go back to being happy. Five years ago, I was happy."

The thing about happiness in the past is that it's in the past. It's just a memory. Yesterday was never here, and tomorrow will never be. We have now. Only now makes a difference. Happiness is not a destination; it is a journey. Many people, as well as my clients, say: "As soon as I get [insert want/desire here], I will be happy."

I have news for you. No, you won't! You won't ever be happy if you pin all your hopes on something that hasn't happened or keep chasing the next dopamine high. People are so eager to live their future lives they forget to live now. Let me give you a quick breakdown of how I know this. Every time I have completed a project, achieved a goal, passed a qualification, saved 'X' amount of money, earned 'X' amount of money and so on, there is a highly temporary feeling of euphoria for about a week.

Now what?

Oh shit, I still have to wake up at 5am for the gym, go to work, make YouTube content, coach my clients, find time for family and friends, pay my bills, write this fucking book, and have enough energy to give a fuck about happiness.

Sounds mundane, right?

Well, yeah, it is. Life is mundane, with little waypoints of rest and adventure. That big thing you're working towards… maybe that 60-inch OLED TV or a date with a Brad Pitt like gigachad or hot blonde, are just waypoints in our lives. This is normal and this is okay.

Finding happiness in the mundane is so important. But the things don't come for free. Holidays, homeware, or hobbies don't come without sacrifices. For most people, it means working 40+ hours a week, or living pay cheque to pay cheque, hoping to fuck they have enough left over to save. A holiday might be two years away, and it's likely to only be for a week or two, so what the fuck are you going to do with your time? Stay miserable and keep telling yourself, "I'll be happy when I am on holiday", or abandon that bullshit and start appreciating the little things? If your bills are paid, there's a roof over your head, food in your belly, family around you, friends to depend on, and hobbies, you are better off than most people.

We live in such an abundant time. Most of us have very little to complain about. Yet unhappiness and depression seem to be at an all-time high. We are conditioned to believe more is better and happiness is the goal. We are all imperfect and should embrace the fact that we don't have to be happy all the time because it's the perfect catalyst to grow and evolve.

> "The only thing that can ever truly destroy a dream is to have it come true."
>
> – Mark Manson, *Everything is F*cked: A Book About Hope*

What if you gain what you think will make you happy? What then? We need purpose. My mother complains about everything she does for the family, but she fucking loves it. Her purpose is to mother the shit out of me and my siblings. It's a nine-on-the-Richter-scale annoying, but now I just let her do it because it makes her happy. She will protest how she does so much for the family, takes a few days to rest, and then complains about being bored. My purpose when writing this is to help people through their breakups. It's hard work, and it can drain the fuck out of me, but I cannot express how great I feel when I am on the phone with a client at 1am (because of a time difference), and they tell me, "Thanks for listening. Thanks for giving me a safe space, and thanks for the advice. I feel better today, and I feel like I will be okay."

That's my happiness. It's not buying shit or going on expensive trips. It's not my romantic relationship. It's doing the day-to-day well and fucking appreciating the sun rising every morning. Anything beyond this is negotiable, including my romantic relationships.

So, you can use romance to enhance your happiness but don't let it be the primary source. You have everything you need right now to be happy, don't fucking waste or abuse it.

SITTING IN THE MUD

I was listening to Simon Sinek on a podcast called *The Diary Of A CEO*. It's my favourite podcast, and the host, Steven Barlett, is a fucking legend. I usually have the podcast on at 5am when I am in the gym. Fuck you if you're judging me for not listening to music when I am training. I am getting my mental muscle on, as well as my guns.

Simon said something that resonated with me. I will butcher the quote, but it's the gist.

"I need someone to sit in the mud with me. I don't need them to fix me or clean me off or give me a towel. I just need them to sit in the mud with me so I don't feel alone when I am sitting in the mud."

— Simon Sinek, *I Feel Lonely*

Mind-fucking-blown! So many friendships and relationships would be better if people did this. Many relationships would be more functional and happy. Simply listening and providing your partner with company can be enough. It can also be the difference between happily ever after or joining me in a breakup coaching session.

If there is one thing I truly fucking regret in my relationship it is that I didn't know how to listen to understand. I would listen to respond. I would wait for my turn to talk. I would try to fix my ex's issues. She never wanted solutions. She just wanted me to listen. Ironically, I very seldom find potential romantic partners who can sit in the mud with me and hold a safe space without trying to fix my shit. The ironic justice of my ex wanting that from me is now what I crave.

So, when I say our exes teach us lessons, this was a very painful and sobering lesson. I have come to understand it's not about winning an argument; it's about engaging and understanding. I wanted to win every little fucking argument because my fragile little ego couldn't handle being wrong. I wanted to be the man, the leader, the alpha, but a true leader doesn't have to tell everyone they're the leader. A true leader will serve those around them without expectation of anything in return. A true leader will listen to understand. A true leader doesn't always have to be right. A true leader will sit in the mud with you. A true leader eats last. Go check out Simon's book *Leaders Eat Last*. It's a great read.

I started writing this book January 2022. As I type these words, it is Sunday, 2nd of April 2023. My anxiety is high because I find myself still single almost three years post-breakup. Although I've had a few minor relationships since then, my breakup from three years ago is still the big one. I like single life. Actually, I fucking love single life. It has afforded me many opportunities and adventures.

The reason my anxiety is high is, firstly, because this is the end of the book and I need to find another project to focus on. Secondly, I have recently dated many women and fooled around. Thirdly, those I dated seriously did not develop into romantic relationships. They were all good women, and I cared for them, but none were right for me. I feel anxious because the latest breakup was very recent, and I don't feel good about it. We were friends at first and then became romantic. Sadly, I wasn't feeling a romantic connection with her.

If there is one thing I have learned, it is not to stay in it if you're not feeling it. You will only resent each other, and it'll end up an ugly breakup.

As it will likely be primarily dumpees reading this, I want you to know I do not feel good about this recent breakup, even though I am the dumper. I wanted to be in love with the woman in question, but we didn't vibe on that level. I still love and care for her as a friend, but sometimes, you're only meant to be friends.

The build-up to our ending was brutal because I didn't want to hurt her. I spent days agonising over what to say. If I let it go on, I would give her false hope and not give her the best version of me. The truly crazy thing is, five years ago, I would've stayed with any woman who gave me attention because I was terrified of being alone. If I didn't have a woman to validate me, I would freak out because I couldn't validate myself.

My pain today is that I can't just settle for the next woman who comes along. I've healed the emotional wounds which festered many years ago. However, solving old issues inevitably creates new ones. Holding myself to better standards and metrics means I am actively choosing to be by myself at a time in my life when I have more romantic options than ever before. My standards for myself have vastly improved. I will likely be single for a little longer, and that's okay.

It can be lonely, but it is on my terms, and I will take that over being with the wrong woman.

Even now, I am in recovery. I am processing feelings over this recent breakup, and I still think about my ex from three years ago from time to time. I am in a vastly better place, a better man, and my mindset has dramatically improved. However, there are days like today when I do not feel okay, and so the journey of recovery continues.

I have tried to make this book as real as possible. I have done my best to be unbiased, but like everyone else, I am the hero in my own story. At the very least, I hope you have acquired some new knowledge to help you navigate your way through the clusterfuck that is a breakup.

My journey has had some of life's best and worst experiences. My breakup destroyed me but also made me into something I never imagined. I never thought I would be coaching people through their breakups, let alone writing a fucking book about them. I am very different from the man I was and am hugely thankful for the path the breakup put me on. If I can recover and make a fucking coaching business out of some of the worst experiences of my life, imagine what you can do. I am no one special, and I am not exceptional at anything. Apart from eating my body weight in chocolate, I'm pretty fucking epic at that.

If you take anything away from this book, take these two things:

1. You will never be happy if you believe happiness is a destination. Your happiness is here and now. You have everything you need to create happiness. What runs parallel with this is pain. Without pain or struggle, there is no growth, which means no happiness. You can only try to choose good pain over bad. Or, at the very least, choose how you respond to pain.

2. You are responsible for everything in your life. Own anything and everything that happens to you like you meant for it to happen. No matter if someone fucks you over. Don't blame the world, don't blame the person who did it, and don't blame the dog next door. By blaming them, you're giving your power away and diminishing your value. Don't give the pricks the satisfaction, and don't let them live rent-free in your head.

Your ex was the best teacher you could hope for. The lesson is painful, but how you use it depends on you.

CHAPTER 10

Surrender

A breakup is a terminal diagnosis that will give you new life and make you stronger if you let it be. Surrendering to the truth of the situation is savagely painful, but it is a pain you must harness. Pain is a wise teacher. It is there not to hurt you, but to guide you towards a solution. The pain from touching a hot stove teaches us not to touch a hot stove again. The pain of a breakup is far more painful, and you may take it as a warning to never get into a romantic relationship again.

However, if you take anything away from this book, it should be that a breakup will teach you things about yourself you never thought possible. It will teach you what not to do next time. It will teach you what you don't want from future partners, and it will teach you to only focus on the things you can control.

Many of us, me included, sit in the breakup mud for too long because it is less painful than heeding the lesson pain is trying to teach us. The pain will go away when we choose to hear the lesson. There are three questions to ask yourself post-breakup, to begin your recovery journey.

1. How did you contribute to the breakup?

2. Did you neglect your own needs in the relationship, and why?

3. Who do you need to become to attract the partner you want?

Answering these three questions will help you take responsibility for your actions, but most importantly put emphasis on you to respond in a healthier way to your feelings, rather than shitting all over the floor and doing something crazy, like stalking your ex. They will help you to understand where you abandoned yourself.

Lastly, they will help you to develop self-love and boundaries so you can attract someone who is a better reflection of you.

You may well be a victim of a breakup and some horrible shit not covered in this book, but you don't have to play the role of a victim. Someone's actions towards you is a reflection of them. There isn't anything you can do about that. You can't love their traumas out of them. You can however ask why was I attracted to that? You can ask why did I allow myself to be treated that way? You can ask why did I stay for as long as I did?

And you can certainly tell yourself that you don't ever have to tolerate that bullshit from anyone ever.

Taking responsibility doesn't excuse your ex-partner's actions, but it certainly neutralises their effect on you, putting the power back in your hands. I am not for one moment saying this is easy, but I am saying you can fucking choose the road, door, portal or whatever the fuck you want to call it, that gets you out of the breakup mud, that breaks you up from your breakup and into recovery. We are all heading towards the same place. We will all end up dead one day, but I choose to get there the way I fucking want to get there. I choose to do my best and be as happy as possible with or without a romantic partner. That can only be achieved if we own our shit and fuck everything else off that we can't control.

My editor has told me to summarise the chapters. I've been writing this book for a while, I'm pretty fucking tired and I'm quite naturally lazy. So, fuck summarising every chapter, I'll just say this. Every chapter in this book comes down to three things.

1. My personal experience: what I learned and passing it on to you.

2. Taking responsibility for everything that happens to you: choose not to be a victim.

3. Let go of the shit out of your control: focus on the shit you can control.

None of the above is original thinking. All I have done is taken the advice from other books that helped me and applied it to getting through a breakup.

My editor has also been nagging me regarding, over-quoting other books. But it's my book so I can do whatever the fuck I want. I can only imagine the comments she will leave on this section. I think I secretly like annoying her. All jokes aside, this book and my breakup journey are a combination of too many resources to mention.

I want to leave you with some other book suggestions that not only help soothe my pain, but heavily influenced my mindset, this book and me 2.0:

- *The Obstacle Is The Way* by Ryan Holiday
- *The Power of TED* by David Emerald
- *The Subtle Art of Not Giving A Fuck* by Mark Manson
- *Atomic Habits* by James Clear
- *How to Not Die Alone* by Logan Ury
- *No More Mr. Nice Guy* by Dr Robert Glover
- *The Gift of Fear* by Gavin de Becker
- *Start with Why* by Simon Sinek

I could go on but that should be enough to get you rolling down the road of recovery. Ironically, none of these books have to do with breakups, except for Power of TED. They are mostly philosophy driven or a shift in mindset.

One last resource that may help you before you put this book down, and that's me. My small but modest YouTube channel, The Love Fix, has over two hundred videos on how to get over a breakup, and over one million views for the channel. My private Facebook recovery group has over twenty thousand people on their recovery journeys. My team and I are in there every day answering your questions and we do live Q&A

sessions. Lastly, my one-to-one breakup recovery coaching sessions. I've coached close to five hundred people at the time of writing, and it has been an immense pleasure to have helped so many to heal and move on to better things. This all started as a way to deal with my breakup pain. It gave me purpose, and helping you to find solutions to your problems, allowed me to find solutions to my problems.

THANK YOU AND ACKNOWLEDGEMENTS

I wanted to make this book all about me because I love the sound of my own voice and I narcissistically admire my own work. But the truth is, my recovery and this book would not be possible without the fucking legendary support of my nearest and dearest.

To my parents. No matter how badly I've ever fucked up or how much pain I was in, they have always been there without fail and unconditionally. They drive me fucking crazy sometimes, but they have always been a source of strength and I love them dearly.

To my siblings, nieces and nephews. I love you all dearly. Life can keep us away from each other and we're probably not as close as I would like, which I very much have a part to play in as I can get buried in my work. I can always count on you and am always here for you.

To my best friends, Joe, Chris and Gopal. Fucking legends! They've walked every heartbreak with me, and I could not wish for better men to be in the trenches with me. I have known these good men for over 20 years, and we've had some crazy adventures together. I cannot imagine my life without you fuckers and I love you all.

To my ex-girlfriend, J. Thank you for the relationship we had together. I value the time we had and the lessons I've learned. You're a good woman, a good mother and I have no hard feelings towards you. We haven't spoken in four years but maybe one day you'll read this book and either laugh or stab me with a spoon. I hope you, your daughter, and your family are healthy and happy. We had a lot of fun together.

To my dog Kenzie who passed away in May 2022. You were there for me in my darkest hours during the first part of the breakup. You wouldn't leave my side and you sat in the mud with me. My heart shattered the day you died, and I don't think it will ever be the same again. I loved every dog I have ever had but I loved you just a little bit more. You were such a unique and special soul; my life is less without you. RIP my son, I will forever miss you.

To my drumming coach, Ciara. What a fucking legend! You have no idea how much your time, effort and lessons helped me when I felt at my lowest. I've loved every lesson we have had together and here's to many more. Keep rocking and never lose your passion and your delightfully simple way of teaching.

To my Love Fix Facebook group friends: Sagi, Tomasz, Lizzy, Tamas, Milo, Andy, David, Callum, Jennifer, Stella. Some of you I have met in person, and I have come to depend on your counsel as amazing online friends.

ENDNOTES

1   Manson, Mark. *The Subtle Art of Not Giving a Fuck: A Counterintuitive Approach to Living a Good Life.* First HarperLuxe edition. New York, NY, HarperLuxe, an imprint of HarperCollinsPublishers, 2018.

2   Boros, Gábor. "Concepts of Love in the 17th Century". *The Culture of Love in China and Europe.* Leiden, The Netherlands: Brill, 2019. https://doi.org/10.1163/9789004397835_009 Web.

3   Bartels, Andreas; Zeki, Semir. The neural basis of romantic love. NeuroReport 11(17):p 3829-3834, November 27, 2000.

4   Wu, Katherine. "Love, Actually: The Science behind Lust, Attraction, and Companionship." *Science in the News*, Harvard University, 14 Feb. 2017, sitn.hms.harvard.edu/flash/2017/love-actually-science-behind-lust-attraction-companionship/.

5   SITNFlash. "Love, Actually: The Science behind Lust, Attraction, and Companionship." *Science in the News*, 19 June 2020, sitn.hms.harvard.edu/flash/2017/love-actually-science-behind-lust-attraction-companionship/.

6   Banschick M.D., Mark. "The High Failure Rate of Second and Third Marriages | Psychology Today United Kingdom." *Www.psychologytoday.com*, www.psychologytoday.com/gb/blog/the-intelligent-divorce/201202/the-high-failure-rate-of-second-and-third-marriages#:~:text=Key%20points. Accessed 30 Oct. 2023.

7   *Divorce statistics 2021: How many UK marriages end in divorce?* (2021) *Scribbler*. Available at: https://www.scribbler.com/Blog/Divorce-Statistics/ (Accessed: 30 October 2023).

8   BARNETT, ROSALIND C., et al. "Adult Son-Parent Relationships and Their Associations with Sons' Psychological Distress." *Journal of Family Issues*, vol. 13, no. 4, Dec. 1992, pp. 505--525, https://doi.org/10.1177/019251392013004007.

9   Artz LMFT, Nicole . "What Is Narcissistic Collapse?" *Choosing Therapy*, 9 May 2023, www.choosingtherapy.com/narcissistic-collapse/#:~:text=Narcissistic%20collapse%20occurs%20when%20a,out%2C%20or%20harm%20to%20others. Accessed 6 Nov. 2023.

10   Bowlby, J. (1969). *Attachment and Loss, Vol. 1: Attachment*. Attachment and Loss. New York: Basic Books.

11   Murray, Henry A. "Analysis of the Personality of Adolph Hitler ." *Analysis of The Personality of Adolph Hitler*, Cornell University Library, Oct. 1943, digital.library.cornell.edu/catalog/nur01134.

Printed in Great Britain
by Amazon